GET OVER YOURSELF; GOD'S HERE!

GET OVER YOURSELF; GOD'S HERE!

A FORTY-DAY JOURNEY of REPENTANCE

KATE MOOREHEAD

ST. MARK'S PRESS

www.stmarkspress.net

WICHITA, KANSAS

St. Mark's Press
8021 W 21st St N
Wichita, KS 67205-1743

Phone:	1-800-365-0439
Email:	stmarkspress@gmail.com
For orders and information:	www.stmarkspress.net

Unless otherwise indicated, Scripture quotations are from the *New Revised Standard Version of the Bible*, copyright © 1989, by the Division of Christian Education of the National Council of the Churches of Christ in the United States of America. Used by permission.

Cover Design: Catherine Lewis, The Exchange (thexchange@cox.net)
Interior Design: J. Ted Blakley

ISBN 10: 0-9618-1128-5
ISBN 13: 978-0-9618-1128-0

This book is dedicated
to
St. James Episcopal Church
in
Wichita, Kansas.

For my eyes have seen Your salvation.
LUKE 2:30

Table of Contents

Ash Wednesday to Saturday

Jesus walked into the desert alone to face the devil. What does it mean for us that he confronted evil before he began his ministry? How can we face and defeat our own temptations? Before we can help anyone else, we must know ourselves and how temptation expresses itself in our own lives. We must face the bad stuff first.

First Week in Lent

How do we hear God's voice in this broken and busy world? Listening for God's voice involves taking time alone, understanding what Jesus taught about the workings of the human mind, and being willing to change our thoughts and opinions.

Chapter 3. Build Healthy Relationships...........43
Second Week in Lent

Our relationships are a vital part of our salvation. Spirituality is not just about prayer; it is about relationships. How can we learn to get along with one another? What does Jesus teach us about relationships?

Chapter 4. Communicate with Others...........65
Third Week in Lent

Jesus faced conflict. He expressed emotion publicly. He got really mad! How does God want us to communicate with each other and with God?

What does it mean to be truly honest with yourself and with others?

Chapter 5. Form Godly Habits
Fourth Week in Lent

Jesus taught us a lot about eating and about money. Working these issues out in our lives can make us so much more balanced and peaceful! He also gave us permission to be late sometimes and to be lonely, too.

Chapter 6. Live in Community
Fifth Week in Lent

Jesus lived in a small group community. If we are going to follow in his footsteps, we must learn to put ourselves last, to get feedback, to forgive and to celebrate each other. The only way to imitate Jesus fully is to live our lives in community.

Chapter 7. Hold On
Holy Week

In the end, Jesus did not want to punish us, he wanted to hold us. And rather than wallowing in our mistakes, we must focus on being his hands and feet in this broken world.

Chapter 8. Prepare for Eternal Life............**153**
Easter Week

We cannot experience the resurrection life if we do not love God. These last few meditations explore what it means to die and then to live again, and how the existence of eternal life changes us now.

Conclusion............**177**

Author's Preface

God truly is here, just waiting for you to open your eyes. Take your mind off yourself and be free. I hope that this book gives you some help as you take your first steps into a life of repentance. It is a life of true beauty and gratitude as you move out of yourself and into God's presence.

May Jesus bless you as you turn these pages.

Kate Moorehead +
October 2009

So long, self;
Well, it's been fun,
But I have found somebody else.

FROM "SO LONG SELF" BY MERCYME

Introduction

When I use the word SIN these days, no one seems to understand what I'm talking about. People sit in my office and stare at me with blank expressions. Maybe they think I am telling them that God is angry with them for a particular behavior or, worst case scenario, that they are simply a lost cause. The word *sin* has been stretched to the point that we hardly know what it means anymore. It has been made to fit our inadequacies, our failures, our misdemeanors, and even our felonies. *Sin* carries so much baggage that I think some people simply shut down when they hear it. Believing that one word doesn't cut it, we've found lots of other words besides plain old *sin* to describe all the stuff that separates us from God. Let me describe a handful of these words for you.

Sometimes I talk to people about their ISSUES. Everyone has *issues.* That's a good word. I can just see people nodding and smiling in my office when I talk about our issues. Having issues is very palatable and acceptable in today's culture.

MISTAKES is another word used to talk about sin. Some mistakes are small; some are huge. Maybe we use this word to get ourselves off the hook, as in, "It was *just* a mistake." *Deliberate mistakes* might be a better way to put it. But still, mistakes doesn't cut it when we are talking about someone deliberately hurting another person.

ADDICTION is a popular word for a particular kind of sin, the kind that you know is wrong but are, nevertheless, almost powerless to stop. It's the kind of sin that is mainly against your own self or your own body but, in turn, wounds everyone who loves you.

And then there is the worst kind of sin. I'm talking about the kind of behavior that seriously damages your own soul, like murder and adultery and other really bad stuff. For these things, perhaps there is no better label than plain old SIN.

Beyond that use of sin, there are EVILS and HORRORS that defy words and understanding.

How can one word encompass all these distinctions? Surely there are different types and degrees of sin. Jesus also spoke of transgression, debt and unrighteousness, but these words have become obsolete to us. So we are left with the word *sin*. Why has it become so difficult to translate and understand what Jesus was trying to tell us? Should we come up with more words to describe the ways that we separate ourselves from God? No, this would only lead to a greater focus on the negative.

Instead, maybe God wants us to honestly acknowledge those things that we have done to separate ourselves and make a straightforward assessment of them, without turning each "sin" into a sacred cow that draws all of our focus and energy.

Harping on the intricacies of our sinfulness is not the best form of repentance. In fact, it can become its own kind of sin, an obsession with self. And we all know how seductive that can be. After all, we love to focus on ourselves. How much time do you spend thinking about how you are feeling or how you look or what people think of you? Thinking about ourselves can take up a lot of our time and energy.

Jesus says that once we repent and turn toward the Light, God forgives us, and our sin is gone. Finished. Over. Poof! *It is as if the sin never existed.* So there must be another way of repentance besides this obsessive, backward-looking focus on what we've done wrong. Sure, we have to look at ourselves in order to make changes, but more importantly, we have to look ahead of us to where we're going.

Jesus calls to all of us with these words, "Repent, for the kingdom of God is at hand!" (cf. Mark 1:15; Matt 3:2, 4:17). A few years ago, I began to spend serious time thinking about what repentance really means. I came up with a new translation that speaks to our current times. When Jesus talked about repentance, what I think he was really saying was:

Get over yourselves!

The Greek word used in the New Testament for repentance is *metanoia.* If *paranoia* is having a distorted mind that is preoccupied with self and how others view us, then *metanoia* is having a changed mind that turns towards God and away from ourselves. In other words,

Get over yourselves! God's here!

So here's my proposal. Since Lent is traditionally a forty-day period in which we are supposed to examine our sins, and since we are not even clear about what the word *sin* means anymore, and since we tend to focus on ourselves to the exclusion of God, let's try something new. Instead of obsessively analyzing what *doesn't* work about ourselves, let's look at what *did* work in Jesus. Maybe when Jesus told us to repent, he was not asking us to over-analyze our wrongdoings but, instead, to turn to him for guidance so that we could be renewed in God.

Jesus was the only man who was born and lived without sin. This was God's Son come down to earth to show us how to live. So let's talk about *Jesus*, and let's talk about what *Jesus* did right. Let's look at how he prayed, how he made decisions, how he communicated. Let's examine all that good stuff and see if it will change our lives. Perhaps instead of beating ourselves up for all the things that we do wrong, we could begin by seeing what Jesus did right and trying to imitate his way of doing things. Maybe this new approach could get us out of the ruts of self-absorption and self-analysis that are so prevalent in our time and culture.

So let's get over ourselves. Let's shift our focus to Jesus' way of doing things and get into a vibrant life with God. Let's begin a journey of repentance.

CHAPTER 1

Face the Bad Stuff First

Ash Wednesday to Saturday

Identify Your Temptations

Jesus, full of the Holy Spirit, returned from the Jordan and was led by the Spirit in the wilderness, where for forty days he was tempted by the devil. He ate nothing at all during those days, and when they were over, he was famished.

LUKE 4:1-2

Britney Spears has everything: great looks, talent, and more money than some small countries. She has everything that we think we need. And she is miserable.

The actor Heath Ledger died at twenty-eight. His recipe for death? Great looks, incredible talent, and lots of money. Despite having "it all" he couldn't sleep at night, so he started taking drugs. And he took too many.

It strikes me that human beings are like my dog Benjamin. Ben is a chocolate lab. He's sweet, but dumb as a rock. If I gave him a fifteen pound bag of dog food, he would gorge himself to death. He would eat until he died. That dog has no idea when to say when.

When it comes to issues of money, good looks, and power, we don't know when to say when either. We think we would be happy if we could just get the fat off our thighs or erase the wrinkles from our eyes. If only we had more money, more influence, better looks, or more friends. If only people noticed us.

We look to the celebrities as if they are minor gods. We call them *the stars*, as if they are lights for us to see by. Kirk Franklin, the popular Christian artist, raps, "America has no more stars, now we call them idols." But look at them, these stars and idols. They are miserable.

What are temptations? They are the urges that draw us away from God. Jesus had three archetypal temptations, but most of us have more like twenty-five (or 500). Jesus said, "No," to his temptations. Most of *us* buy right into them and live according to their advice, . . . until we realize our lives aren't working.

What are your temptations? Since I work and have three small boys, one of mine is this (and it's a good one), "Poor me! I work *so* hard. No one works as hard as I do!"

Or, there's a guy I know who's a shopaholic. His temptation? "If I buy more things, I will feel better." He had racked up enormous credit card debt buying little trinkets and stuff that he thought he needed. He ended up owing more than he could pay and was evicted from his apartment. A friend built him a wooden trailer that he stuffed full of his belongings. While he was on the road to his mother's house, the trailer broke apart on the highway. It was so full of stuff that it literally exploded, and his things were scattered across the road. So he called me, and he said, "It's not fair! Why is God so unfair to me?"

I have another friend who truly believes that she needs a man to make her happy. After years of failed relationships, she has decided that all the men who love her will leave her. And so they do leave her, and she gets sucked deeper into the vortex of her own temptation. Every relationship she endures only seems to prove her theory that all men will leave her. She finds herself alone, and her temptation becomes her reality.

What are your temptations? Do they tell you that you are not good enough? That you are stupid? That you are ugly? That you are a failure? Do they tell you that it's okay to drink alcohol even though your dad drank himself to death? Do they tell you that this person you've just met is *the one*, even though he hits you? Do they tell you that you can't make it because you haven't gotten *the break* that you need?

The best thing to do with temptations is to take them out and look at them. That's what Jesus did. He sat alone in the quiet, and he let the enemy speak to him. He listened to the devil, to the tempter himself. Only then could he clearly say, "No!"

Write down your temptations, and then read them aloud. Tell someone about them. Bring them into the light. You will be amazed at how ridiculous many of them are, and how easy it is not to buy into them if you just speak them aloud. Spend time alone like Jesus did and discover how destructive your thoughts have become. And then—only then—will they begin to lose their power over you. Oh, they will return, but next time you will be able to recognize them more quickly. You will not be so taken in.

If only my friend could realize the foolishness of her temptation. If only she could see how her believing that every man who loves her leaves her brings that reality to pass, she could be so incredible. She could be happy. Maybe she could actually find time to love herself. If only my shopaholic friend could realize that things can't make him feel full, he might begin to fully live. If only I could see that my job and my children are blessings from God and not busyness to overcome, I could enjoy my life in deeper ways.

We must get out of the muck of our self-centeredness if we are ever to truly live. The last thing that the tempter wants is for you to realize who you really are—a child of God, beloved and capable of infinite possibilities.

Lean on God

The tempter came and said to Jesus, "If you are the Son of God, command these stones to become loaves of bread." But Jesus answered, "It is written, 'One does not live by bread alone, but by every word that comes from the mouth of God.'"

MATTHEW 4:3–4

Of all the people to have walked the earth, Jesus was certainly the most capable. He could do anything for himself and for others. Just the sound of his voice or the touch of his hand could radically change lives. Imagine having that kind of power! No wonder temptation came to Jesus first in the form of self-reliance. What a great temptation for a supremely capable man. The problem for the devil, however, was this: Jesus knew that, for all his capabilities, he needed his heavenly Father. Jesus knew that his power flowed directly from the Father, which gave him the strength to overcome this temptation.

Unfortunately, most of us live our lives in total obedience to the temptation of self-reliance. Why should we ask God for help when we can be in charge of our own lives? Instead of recognizing our dependence on God, we opt for the do-it-yourself life, believing that we can somehow control our universe. We fool ourselves into thinking that we can make our own success, solve our own problems, and create our own happiness. I think the wealthy and the young are the most susceptible to this kind of temptation.

We use a variety of means in our futile attempts to control our world. We schedule every moment of our lives, as if the order we create will keep chaos at bay. We alter our moods through drugs or alcohol. We try to influence the behavior of others, sometimes with manipulation.

Maybe you've seen the bumper sticker that says, "Jesus Is Coming. Look Busy." Among other things, I think that bumper sticker is poking fun at our belief that we control our lives and that Christ's coming might actually throw a wrench into our plans. In truth, a more accurate bumper sticker might read, "God's Here. Look Busy." That's what most of us do every day of our lives.

Everything about our culture tells us that we can be in control of our world. Buy this product, and you will be happy. Take this vitamin, and you will stay young. Make enough of an effort, and you will succeed in life. Take this vacation, and you will find relaxation. Buy this life insurance policy, and everything will be alright.

The antidote to this kind of temptation, ironically, is suffering. When our lives fall apart, the mirage of this temptation starts to crack, and we realize that we were never really in control of our lives. The truth is that we fall ill, loved ones die, stock markets crash, and we have very little idea about what is going to happen to us tomorrow. The more we learn about the universe, the more we realize how fragile we are as a human race. We hurtle through space on this tiny planet, in a small area of atmospheric pressure. The very fact of our existence is truly miraculous. When compared to the Maker of the universe, we are insignificant. God says to each of us, "Remember that you are dust, and to dust you will return" (cf. Gen 3:19).

The temptation to be completely self-reliant is a great one, but the truth is that you and I are fragile beings who cannot even breathe without God. Everything that we do, we do by the grace of God. We must remember this. We are not capable of living without God. Jesus knew it. And that's how he lived every day of his earthly life.

Don't Worship Anything Else But God

Then the devil led Jesus up and showed him in an instant all the kingdoms of the world. And the devil said to him, "To you I will give their glory and all this authority; for it has been given over to me, and I give it to anyone I please. If you, then, will worship me, it will all be yours."

LUKE 4:5–7

The second temptation was even more powerful than the first. In it, the evil one upped the ante. No longer was he talking about mere food. No, this was bigger and better. The second offer made to Jesus is one that is made to us every day of our lives, "Worship me and you can have everything the world can offer." But Jesus knew this: focus on the wrong thing, and you subtly but *powerfully* remove yourself from God.

The evil one takes many forms. Money is a favorite one, so is success, passion, popularity, and fame. In order to understand your own struggle with the tempter, ask yourself, "What is my first priority in life?" Is it God? If not, you've got an *issue*!

John joined our parish after he had a heart attack. He had gone to a top-notch college with the belief that his life's purpose was to rise above the poverty that had enveloped his parents. He graduated with honors and went to work at a top-paying corporation. He married and had kids, but spent all his time working, telling himself this was his way of loving his family. "They will never be poor. They will never have to hurt like I did." That was the thought that ran through his mind when he missed baseball games, family vacations, and time alone with his wife.

At forty-five, after pulling eighty-hour work weeks for years, he suffered a massive heart attack. Lying in the hospital bed, he woke up for the first time in many years. He realized that somehow he had come to worship success and, in doing that, had sold his soul and almost lost his life.

The transition from worship of the wrong thing to truly living was difficult for John. He realized he couldn't simply cut back at work. He realized that, in fact, there was very little about his work that he found fulfilling. He resigned.

John and his family had to move into a smaller house. They had to reevaluate their lifestyle. John had to face that old demon that told him he was making his children suffer whenever he could not afford to buy them what they wanted. But he was also able to see that his children were happier. They may have had less stuff, but they had a dad for the first time in their lives.

John ended up resurrecting an old, childhood hobby. He remembered he had gifts that he had neglected for years. He became a master carpenter, and his wife, who was not finding fulfillment at home alone, found herself a job as a teacher.

They struggled a bit, but they also found balance and a level of fulfillment that they had not known before. And John began to come to church. He said to me, "I feel alive for the first time in many years. It's as if I had handed my soul to that company. I am so grateful to have a second chance."

Jesus asked, "What good is it if you gain the whole world but lose your soul?" (cf. Matt 16:26). Let me ask you this: Where are your priorities? Where do you expend most of your physical and mental energies? Are you worshiping something that ultimately brings death? Or, are your eyes fixed on the One who brings life?

Evil Is Muddy

When the woman saw that the fruit of the tree was good for food and pleasing to the eye, and also desirable for gaining wisdom, she took some and ate it.

GENESIS 3:6

There are too many tragedies, too much pain and needless suffering in this world, for us not to take seriously the existence of evil. There must be some other force, something antithetical to God, that lures us away. Eve did not come up with the idea of eating the forbidden fruit. That idea, that temptation, was introduced to her by a source outside herself. That darkness was somehow already in existence, waiting to be destructive.

The motivations of people in this world are complex. I see parishioners hurt themselves and others, and yet, I would not say that they were fundamentally *bad* people. Many times they are very faithful Christians. But despite their efforts to control destructive behavior, these people succumb to temptation and do the very things they try to avoid.

I perform weddings that are nothing short of a battlefield, full of soap-opera drama and power struggles, the dreams of an idyllic wedding, . . . lost. The children's home near our church is full of teenage boys who have been abandoned. Many arrive in police cars, their parents having abused them, the dreams of parents and children for a loving family, . . . lost. I know people who, after years of sobriety, begin to drink again, the dreams of a life of wholeness, . . . lost.

A few months ago a woman came to visit me. A Roman Catholic, she was married and having an affair, which she had no intention of ending. Somehow she thought that, because I married a couple who had each been divorced, I would understand what she called her *predicament* and encourage her to divorce her husband. The man she had been sleeping with was begging her to end her marriage, stating that her love had rescued him from depression. She told herself that she was actually helping this man, saving him with her love. She acted as if her affair was some kind of romance novel and that she was doing something wonderful by loving a man who was not her husband. The power of her feelings for her lover made her believe that leaving her husband was the loving thing to do. She had become so enveloped in the affair that she could no longer see the destruction that it was causing her soul. She was a very confused woman.

The devil is the personification of everything that ruins us. Why would a woman who described herself as happily married engage in such destruction? Why would she ever begin such an affair? And how could she have come to believe that the affair was good? I'm sure that there were a host of painful incidents in her past, but no matter what the circumstances, she was hurting herself and others.

The problem with the devil is that his existence is not as well differentiated to us as it was to Jesus. Evil exists for us; yes, of that I am sure. But it is woven into the fabric of our lives. The powers of darkness are so complex, so intertwined with our very being, that some choices are nearly impossible to make without choosing wrong. When it comes to the evil that surrounds us, we simply cannot see with the clarity that Jesus possessed. Sometimes avoiding sin is like trying to walk between the raindrops.

I think that is the reason we love action movies like Star Wars. We long for evil to make itself apparent. We love hating Darth Vader. As Vader parades across the set, the ominous music begins to play. He is so easy to identify, so easy to hate! If only we could have it so easy. If only life could be so crystal-clear.

On rare occasion, evil manifests itself with such potency that it is hard to avoid. Hitler is an obvious example. Just think of all the well-meaning Germans who were hoodwinked by him for so many years. Or think of those who averted their eyes because they were afraid or busy or avoided the truth for some other reason that seemed legitimate at the time. Hindsight is 20/20, but even with Hitler standing before them, many people chose to cheer with the crowd rather than question his madness.

Think about this: the fact that Jesus was able to have a verbal, open battle with the devil himself is a sign of the immensity of his wellness. The devil could not inhabit him in the way that he does us. He was forced to be visible. Jesus identified the evil one even before he began his series of temptations, and half the battle was won right there.

I wish that I could bring the devil out of hiding and describe him to you with clarity, but it seems that only Jesus could do that. The rest of us are left living in the muddy waters of the in-between time, when evil is subtly woven into the fabric of our lives, and we must pray before every decision we make and every action we take.

Reflection Questions for Chapter 1

1. What are some of your temptations? What thoughts and urges draw you from the love of God? Write them down. Speak them aloud. Bring the darkness into the light.

2. Evil is muddy and difficult to describe, and yet we are called to state clearly when we are tempted or inclined to turn away from God. Think of times in your life when you turned away from God. What were those times like? How can you learn from them?

CHAPTER 2

Listen for God's Voice

First Week in Lent

Listen for the Shepherd

"My sheep hear my voice. I know them, and they follow me."

JOHN 10:27

I met a woman who heard God's voice. Her daughter had been killed in a car accident. Every day driving to work, she would swear at God and pound the steering wheel of her car. She would use the worst words possible. She was furious about her daughter's death. For two years, she practiced this kind of rage in the car, rage at God. Then one day, she stopped at a light. She raised her fists to pound on the steering wheel, and the voice came to her. It said, "Lean on me." That was it, three words. But the presence of peace was so tangible that everything changed for her in that moment. Everything. Her healing began that day.

Most of us do not hear God's voice so plainly. We have trouble distinguishing the Shepherd's voice from all the others that compete for our attention. Sheep are pretty simple animals, but they know the shepherd's voice and will follow no one else. Like sheep, we can recognize the Good Shepherd's voice, but we must practice the art of listening in order to refine our hearing.

My friend Michael fell into a coma after a routine surgery went terribly wrong. His brain looked dead on the brain scan. Then his wife began to hold his hand and speak to him. She recounted their relationship, from the moment that they met. For twelve hours, she spoke. And he began to listen.

I don't know what she said to him that day. Maybe she recounted to him how they first met in a dingy bar somewhere, how he bothered her for a date. Who knows what she said, but she was talking about her love for him, and he could hear the sound of that love. It woke him up. The doctors and nurses watched as his brain, literally, came back to life.

The voice of the Good Shepherd comes in many and varied ways. Sometimes it comes to us through the voices of those we love or the voice of a wise stranger, sometimes in the sound of music or the blowing of a simple breeze. However it comes, somewhere deep down inside, we know that God is speaking. After all, we are sheep, and, as dumb as sheep are, they do know the voice of their Master. Deep down inside, we know that Voice better than we know our own selves, . . . if only we would listen.

Take Time to Be Alone

They went to a place called Gethsemane;
and Jesus said to his disciples, "Sit here while I pray."

MARK 14:32

Most clergy are required to take a battery of tests before they can be ordained. One of these is the Myers-Briggs indicator. Here, by answering questions, one puts oneself into certain categories: introverted, intuitive, etc. The first category addresses the question of whether one is an introvert or an extrovert. We clergy like to talk about our Myers-Briggs labels. Perhaps we let them define us a bit too much.

I believe that Jesus would have been on the zero line between introvert and extrovert. He seemed to thrive and even derive energy in crowds. He was able to wander the countryside with a following. He relied upon his disciples for support and feedback. Yet he also needed to be alone. Often he would wander away late at night or early in the morning to spend time alone with God.

The human being has to balance an inner life of prayer and thoughts with an outer life of communication and interaction.

Most of us tend toward either introversion or extroversion, needing to be around people to restore our sense of purpose or needing to be alone to recharge our batteries. For Jesus, it seems that both time alone and time with people were vital. He prayed alone, and he attended worship in synagogues. He taught, and he meditated. He found a balance between time alone with God and time serving God in the midst of people. He experienced God with others and when he was alone.

Would Jesus have preferred to stay on the mountain praying? We will never fully know. I believe that he was driven by his love of people and his desire to share the good news of God with them. Sharing the good news was another form of prayer for him, just as essential and life-giving as his time alone.

How balanced is your life? Do you give yourself time with others and time alone? Do you set aside quiet time for God?

Understand Your Own Mind

"The kingdom of heaven may be compared to someone who sowed good seed in his field; but while everybody was asleep, an enemy came and sowed weeds among the wheat, and then went away. So when the plants came up and bore grain, then the weeds appeared as well. And the slaves of the householder came and said to him, 'Master, did you not sow good seed in your field? Where, then, did these weeds come from?' He answered, 'An enemy has done this.' The slaves said to him, 'Then do you want us to go and gather them?' But he replied, 'No; for in gathering the weeds you would uproot the wheat along with them. Let both of them grow together until the harvest; and at harvest time I will tell the reapers, Collect the weeds first and bind them in bundles to be burned, but gather the wheat into my barn.'"

MATTHEW 13:24b–30

There is a point in everyone's life that I call *the awakening*. It usually happens during adolescence, but it can happen earlier if there is trauma, or later if the mental development of a child is stunted. The awakening occurs when one realizes that the world is not quite working like it is supposed to work.

At some point, we realize that life is not fair, that people are mean, self-centered, and ugly. We begin to recognize that things are not working out as we planned and that they may never work out smoothly. C. S. Lewis sometimes described the world as *bent*. Not broken completely, but bent, askew, off. Things are a bit of a mess.

When I was in sixth grade, I began attending a private school. I had come from an inner-city public school where we worked out our problems by beating each other up. When I arrived at the preppy private school, I quickly realized that I did not fit in. The kids there were mean. Each day for a whole week, I was sent home from school for crying uncontrollably. This world was turning out to be harder than I expected, and I didn't know if I could handle it. Part of me wanted to go home to my mom, bury my head in the sand, and try to go back to being oblivious. But I couldn't do that. I had to face life.

This world is made up of wheat and weeds. There is great beauty, great goodness, and a multitude of things that remind us of God. That is the wheat. There is also great injustice, great cruelty, and great pain. These are the weeds. The wheat and the weeds exist both inside us and outside us. The world is a mixed-up place, but what a relief to realize this fact.

The most poignant part of Jesus' parable has to do with the removal of the weeds. The slaves offer to pull them, but the landowner refuses. No, they must co-mingle. They must grow up together, and then, at the end of the age, the reapers will separate them.

It is not our job to get rid of the bad stuff. If we tried, we would hurt each other in the process. Instead we are to wait, cultivate the wheat, and identify the weeds. God will do the judging later; the weed removal is God's job.

The human mind is full of weeds—temptation, distraction, lust, envy—all the stuff that carries our minds away from God. But the mind is also full of love, gratefulness, and joy. Those who meditate teach us to let the wild thoughts exist. Don't try to remove them, or you will become entangled in them. Better to let the weeds be, and gently try to bring yourself back to focusing on the things of God, the wheat.

The kingdom of God is all around us, but it is surrounded and infested by weeds. This parable that Jesus told is like a Zen koan, so full of wisdom that we can meditate on it for years. For the rest of my life, I will be identifying the wheat and the weeds. Doing so is an essential part of understanding myself.

Resist Bible Bullets

Then the devil took him to Jerusalem and placed him on the pinnacle of the temple, saying to him, "If you are the Son of God, throw yourself down from here, for it is written, 'He will command his angels concerning you, to protect you,' and 'On their hands they will bear you up, so that you will not dash your foot against a stone.'"

LUKE 4:9–10

In his final effort to tempt Jesus in the wilderness, the devil quotes Scripture. I have found it quite remarkable that the enemy of God would use Scripture to justify his purpose. If the devil is able to quote Scripture, then we must not simply assume that all those who quote the Bible are in the right. We must think, interpret, listen, and evaluate. We must also pray.

Many Christians use Scripture as a weapon, firing verses at one another in discourse, as if to back oneself up with Scripture is to present the ultimate authority. I like to call these *Bible Bullets*. Often these *Bible Bullets* are taken out of their context. They do not always serve their purpose; they are not necessarily truth.

The Bible is the ultimate authority for Christians and for Jews, but not in a single verse. Unless read in its entirety and placed in its context, the Bible contradicts itself. I believe that God inspired the Bible to be complex and multifaceted for a reason. It is not designed to be used as a weapon or to justify a point. God would not want it used in such a manner. It is meant to be engaged as we would engage in a very important relationship with someone whom we respect and love above all others.

The devil quotes Scripture with the belief that Jesus will destroy himself simply because a single verse of Scripture says so. But Jesus responds in the best way possible. He uses Scripture right back again. He defeats the devil in the language of the devil's own choosing.

Identify God's Voice

". . . and the sheep hear his voice. He calls his own sheep by name and leads them out. When he has brought out all his own, he goes ahead of them, and the sheep follow him because they know his voice."

JOHN 10:3–4

How does one follow Jesus? In this story about the shepherd, Jesus makes a simple point: all we need to do is recognize his voice. This is such a relief to me. We don't have to understand Christ. We don't have to do good works or merit his love in some way. All we need to do is recognize his voice. When we hear the sound of joy, we need to follow its call.

But what does joy sound like? How do we know what is God's voice and what is the voice of our own troubled nature? Discerning the sound of love is truly the goal of this life. What does love look like? What does it sound like? This we need to know if we are to follow Christ. Strangely, the sound of God's voice can be rich and deep, or it can be high and lofty. It can be found in the voice of a woman crying or an old man telling a story. It is buried deep within the sound of our loved ones' calling. It is the best words that we have ever said.

A month or so ago, I had minor surgery. I was a bit scared to be put under. As they wheeled me into the operating room, I felt like a helpless child. I looked into the bright florescent lights, into the faces of nurses and technicians, and wondered if I would be okay. This was not the perspective that I was used to having. Usually I am the one standing, holding someone's hand or saying a prayer. Here, I was the one on the gurney.

When we got to the operating room, they transferred me to the table and spread my arms out at my sides. They put something in my IV to make me sleep. I looked up. A man in his forties was at my head. This is what he said, "Don't you worry, honey. I will take care of you as if you were my own daughter." And he stroked my head.

I went to sleep right after that, but as my mind faded, I thought to myself, "Was that God?" I knew that it was just a man doing his job, but it sounded so much like God to me.

Don't Let Your Guard Down

When the devil had exhausted every test, he departed from Jesus until an opportune time.

LUKE 4:13

This one sentence tells us so much. The temptations would return, even to Jesus. But now that he had identified them, now that he knew what they looked like, perhaps the next encounter with temptation would be easier. The truth is that temptation weaves itself in and out of our existence. There is no driving it away forever. It just waits for a chink in the armor, a moment of weakness, to come back again.

When I was a young adult, I did some intense therapy. After a few years, I felt that I knew my issues, my stuff, my sinfulness. I thought that, in being able to identify these things, I would master them quickly and put them to rest. In retrospect, I have not found that to be the case. I am often shocked by how a bad day, lack of sleep, or even the smallest misfortune can call back all the old demons. Suddenly, I find myself wallowing in self-pity or acting childishly again. The battle never ends.

Our fallen nature does not disappear. It does, though, become more familiar to us over time so that, when it rears its ugly head, we can tell it to go away. Even for Jesus, the devil waited in the wings, looking for an opportunity to invade his mind and drive him from God's purposes.

Remember that you will never rid yourself of temptation entirely in this life. Christians are called to a life of vigilance. We spend time in discernment, examining our decisions and the motivations behind them. Sin can be subtle and slip into the most unexpected places, so we must take good care of ourselves and know ourselves well so that we can resist temptation. So let's not let our guard down.

The Running Father

So he set off and went to his father. But while he was still far off, his father saw him and was filled with compassion; he ran and put his arms around him and kissed him.

LUKE 15:20

When I picture heaven, I think of God as waiting there. I see St. Peter standing at the gates with some kind of clipboard, ready to examine my application. I have imagined entry as an in-or-out kind of matter. Do I merit salvation? Does God want to let me in? God waits, I apply, and I am either accepted or rejected.

Why is this so? Why do we tend to view heaven in an all-or-nothing sort of way? Why do we picture God as stagnant? Maybe the notion of purifying ourselves or somehow meriting God has led us to believe that God sits in judgment. Certainly the book of Revelation paints a picture of Christ seated on a throne, sitting and waiting for us to approach. The largest, most beautiful stained glass window at our church depicts that scene, the God of judgment waiting to decide about us.

In what we call The Parable of the Prodigal Son, Jesus invites us to consider a different picture of God. A parishioner of mine once pointed out that we should call it, *The Parable of the Running Father.* Here, a young man leaves his father, squanders his inheritance, and returns to beg for the wages of a servant. But, as he is approaching his home, his father runs out to meet him. He runs, he embraces, and he celebrates. There is no consideration given to what the young man has done or not done. All that the Father does is celebrate. He pulls out all the stops for his boy who "was dead and is alive again, who was lost and is found" (Luke 15:24).

Of course, there are more aspects to God than we will ever be able to comprehend. Judgment is one aspect, but that is not the one Jesus chooses to express in this parable. No, here we see a Father who runs out to meet his child. This Father runs! He does not leave all the effort to the young man struggling to return. Instead, he meets his son with arms outstretched.

Loren Eiseley, the famous anthropologist and naturalist, was traveling in the Colorado Rockies trying to catch a rare breed of sparrow hawk. He came upon an abandoned stone cottage, the perfect place for such birds to nest. He quietly entered the house and heard some rustling above a bookshelf next to the far window. He pulled up an old chair, lifted himself up, and shined a flashlight on the birds to stun them. He reached out to grab the female, but the male pounced on his hand and began to peck at him furiously. He was forced to let the female go, and she flew out the window. Eiseley then tried to catch the male bird, who put up quite a fight. When he finally succeeded in capturing the little bird, his hand was a bloody mess. He placed the bird in a small black box with air holes in the top. The box was not big enough for the bird to move around. He took his prize back to the camp.

That night, Eiseley couldn't sleep. He kept thinking about the bird, separated from its mate, imprisoned in the box. The next morning, much to his own surprise, he decided to set it free. He took the bird out of the box and placed it on the grass in front of the camp. The bird lay there for a full minute as if it were dead. Then, in a flash, it shot upwards into the sky. At that moment, Eiseley said that he heard a scream, the likes of which he had never heard before. The female sparrow hawk, who had been circling above the camp all night, came hurtling down to meet her mate, screaming. They met and danced in the sky.

What if, when you get to heaven, instead of a gate and a man with a clipboard, you find that God is hurtling down to meet you, screaming with joy? What if you are met by the Running Father, the God who loves you so much that he races up to you, embraces you and celebrates your return? Now that sounds like heaven to me.

Reflection Questions for Chapter 2

1. What do you imagine that God's voice sounds like? How would you be able to identify it?

2. What are some of the weeds that occupy your mind, the thoughts that recur and distract you from God?

3. When are you most susceptible to distraction and temptation? When do you let your guard down?

CHAPTER 3

Build Healthy
Relationships

Second Week in Lent

Listen Closely to the People Who Push Your Buttons

On the third day there was a wedding in Cana of Galilee, and the mother of Jesus was there. Jesus and his disciples had also been invited to the wedding. When the wine gave out, the mother of Jesus said to him, "They have no wine." And Jesus said to her, "Woman, what concern is that to you and to me? My hour has not yet come." His mother said to the servants, "Do whatever he tells you."

JOHN 2:1–5

Is there anything more embarrassing than having your mother join you at a party? Most young men would rather die than have their mom join them for a date. I doubt if this tendency has changed much over the centuries. It is normal for a young man to switch his devotion and attachment from his mother to his friends and peers. When the shift occurs, his mother (though still deeply loved) becomes an annoyance and an embarrassment. I know this. I have three sons.

It says in the Gospel of John that Jesus' mother was present at the wedding party in Cana. I get the impression that she did not tag along with Jesus. The gospel writer simply states that she was there, presumably a guest in her own right. Jesus was there with his disciples, so he must have already begun his teaching. I wonder how he felt about his mother's presence. Here he was, a new rabbi, and his mother was hanging around. The Bible does not go into his feelings about her presence, but it does recount a tense conversation.

Mary gives Jesus what I like to call a *one-liner*. Mothers can say just one sentence, and you know exactly what they mean. The meaning is underneath the words, hidden in the tone and the look. A mother can guilt-trip her child with a glance. With very few words, she can express disappointment or make a request. This is the kind of interaction Mary has with Jesus. She just says four words! "They have no wine" (2:3). That's it. She does not ask Jesus to perform a miracle, but Jesus seems to know exactly what she is asking, and he is angered by her request.

His response is abrupt, "Woman, what concern is that to you and to me? My hour has not yet come" (2:4). He sounds pushed, as if she is requesting something that is not her business. He doesn't think this is the moment. He wants to wait and enjoy the party. How dare she nudge him this way? It isn't the right time.

How motherly for Mary to want to rescue the situation. How much like a mother for her to insinuate that her son might be just the right one to make everything better. But after his annoyed response, she no longer speaks to him. She just directs the servants to follow his orders. She has nudged him.

She has put in her two cents. She leaves the rest to him. Strange to think that Jesus might have had a meddling mother. But isn't it common, almost inevitable, that a loving mother will find it hard to let go when her son grows up?

The best part of this story is that Jesus takes her advice. After grumbling about her interference, he does just what she wanted. And, as it turns out, it *was* the right time. Like so many mothers, Mary was right. Even Jesus needed a nudge to begin his ministry. Even Jesus wanted to wait a little longer, to stay comfortable for just a little longer. Even Jesus held back. Even the Son of God needed encouragement.

I wonder sometimes if God isn't encouraging us through the people who push our buttons. Clearly God spoke to Jesus through his meddling mother at that wedding. What if God also nudges us through the people who annoy us? What if those people whom we can't stand are in fact our best teachers? What if, out of all the people in the world, it is the people who drive us nuts whom we most need to listen to? Perhaps only they can help us change our water into wine.

Give People Permission to Change

When they heard this, all in the synagogue were filled with rage.
They got up, drove him out of the town, and led him to the brow
of the hill on which their town was built, so that they might hurl
him off the cliff. But he passed through the midst of them and
went on his way.

LUKE 4:28–30

Why do we equate Christianity with harmonious relationships?
Members of the Christian family are supposed to get along and
love one another without conflict, yet Jesus' visit to his family's hometown was nothing short of disastrous. Nazareth sits
on a steep hill among cliffs. Falling from one of these cliffs
would most certainly result in death. Imagine what would have
become of the gospel if the people of Nazareth had succeeded
in their mission. Jesus would have died before his ministry
ever really got started!

It seems significant that one of the first places Jesus visits
is the synagogue he grew up attending. Where else do you go
when you come out of the desert? You return to the familiar.
You go home. No doubt Jesus had pictured himself preaching

there. What did it feel like for him to enter the place where he had worshiped for thirty years? Memories must have flooded his mind as he stepped inside. The experience must have seemed strange in all its familiarity, like home can seem when you return to it after having grown up and traveled the world. It must have seemed small to him.

At first the people of Nazareth are friendly. "Isn't this Joseph's son?" they ask (Luke 4:22). They honor him by asking him to read from the scriptures, and he does. He reads the prophet Isaiah, and when he declares that he is the one Isaiah is speaking of, the people don't seem to register his words at all. They think they know him, but their knowledge of him prevents them from really seeing him. They are crippled by their certainty.

I believe that unwavering certainty makes for bad religion. A faith tradition becomes dangerously brittle when it claims to know God completely or to hold the key to secret knowledge missing from all other faith traditions. How essential it is for all people of faith to remember that we know very little! We do not come to God because we know or understand God but because God knows us.

Jesus must have been saddened by his encounter with his home community. If he knew that he could perform no miracles there, why did he return? Was he, like so many of us, homesick for that childhood place of safety and comfort? Was he lonely? Was he just curious? We may never know. We do know that he walked away from Nazareth that day, leaving the familiar behind. From that point on, Jesus did not have a home—not on earth, anyway. For all of us who make the attempt to grow up, perhaps there is no home quite like the ones we had as a child. There is only God, and the struggle to find our way to our real Home.

Grow Up

Then his mother and his brothers came; and standing outside,
they sent to him and called him. A crowd was sitting around
him; and they said to him, "Your mother and your brothers and
sisters are outside, asking for you." And he replied, "Who are
my mother and my brothers?" And looking at those who sat
around him, he said, "Here are my mother and my brothers!
Whoever does the will of God is my brother and sister and
mother."

MARK 3:31–35

Jesus grew up. In psychological terms, he became fully differentiated from his family. He no longer lived his life to please or placate them. He was not governed by their comfort or pleasure. He was truly independent, so much so that an out-of-the-blue request for attention did not seem to upset him.

Most of us would react strongly if our family members came to us in the middle of our ministry and wanted us to come home. Jesus' mother and brothers were wanting him back. They wanted him to stop this dangerous teaching business. In Mark's account, they accuse him of being possessed by a demon. They think he has gone mad! He no longer resembles the Jesus they knew. Like so many families, they are unable to let him grow to his full potential without contemplating some sort of intervention. He must be brainwashed or possessed. This is no longer our baby, our child.

This story of Jesus asserting his independence is essential to the gospels. It is an account of family conflict within the life of God Incarnate. Our American culture portrays ideal family life as being peaceful and free of conflict and disappointment. In reality, the healthiest of families will struggle to acknowledge the growth and development of their adult children. If Jesus were a *nice* man, he would have gone outside, hugged his mom and brothers, and brought them inside for dinner. Worse still, he would have returned home so as not to upset them. But Jesus was not *nice*; he was a lover of God. And God alone knew the ramifications of his ministry and the absolute necessity that he stay the course.

Instead of abandoning the scene to placate his family, Jesus uses the conflict to inspire a lesson. He gives those who sit with him an insight into true intimacy: relationships that weather conflict are stronger, broader, deeper, and more flexible than those that do not. *Who are my mother and my brothers? Those who do the will of God.*

Once a person is totally immersed in God, family becomes those who love God. At its best, the life of a worshiping community is even better than family life. At its best, church community can generate a kind of support that is deeper and larger. Let me explain.

After I birthed each of my three boys, I brought them to church as soon as they were healthy enough to be exposed to the public. As I officiated the services, these babies were literally passed from one set of loving hands to another. I kept my eyes on them, but there always seemed more genuine caretakers available than I had a need for, trustworthy people, people whom I knew and loved. It was like the babies were riding on a wave of support and love that extended far beyond what any one family could give them.

I think that Jesus could conceive of a world in which people were in tune with the will of God. The mutual support and ministry that could occur under such circumstances is mind-boggling. I catch glimpses of it every once in a while in church, when the widow is surrounded by genuine support and prayers, when the elderly woman wakes up to find that someone from the church has left flowers by her hospital bed, when a new mother gets a home-cooked meal delivered to her house. It happens a lot, but what if it happened all the time?

What is family? Is it not the gathering of those who love one another unconditionally? And isn't that just what God wants for us?

Talk About Death

Jesus said, "Little children, I am with you only a little longer. You will look for me; and as I said to the Jews so now I say to you, 'Where I am going, you cannot come.' I give you a new commandment, that you love one another. Just as I have loved you, you also should love one another. By this everyone will know that you are my disciples, if you have love for one another."

Simon Peter said to him, "Lord, where are you going?" Jesus answered, "Where I am going, you cannot follow me now; but you will follow afterward."

JOHN 13:33–36

When Jesus was ready to die, he spoke openly about it. Of course, the disciples didn't understand when he told them that they couldn't follow him where he was going. He told them that he would suffer and die, but they couldn't take that in. He was honest about his coming death. He talked about it. They just couldn't hear him.

How often I see people who won't discuss death. They can be on hospice care with incurable cancer, and still, they refuse to speak of it. Their avoidance of the pain of death only increases the fear of it and causes pain for their loved ones.

How much healthier it is to follow in Jesus' footsteps. Talk about it! After all, the death rate is 100%. So far, none of us have managed to live forever, no matter how many anti-aging products we've used, no matter how hard we've exercise. Death is real. It is unavoidable, and we must speak openly when it approaches.

Take Care of the Ones You Love

When Jesus saw his mother and the disciple whom he loved standing beside her, he said to his mother, "Woman, here is your son." Then he said to the disciple, "Here is your mother."

JOHN 19:26–27

On the cross, Jesus makes sure that his mother will be cared for. He thinks of others. He creates a verbal will of sorts, a plan. Even on the cross, while his lungs are filling with fluid, he speaks these important words in order to make sure that his mother will have a man to look after her.

In biblical times, women were considered worthless without a man. They could be left to starve. It was important to birth a son because only sons could care for a woman in her old age. Jesus made sure that his mother would not be alone. He loved her until the end.

As painful as it is to think of what would happen to your family if you were to die, it is essential that you contemplate this. Creating a plan, a will, a place for your loved ones—your parents, spouse, children—is crucial. Love them enough to speak of your dying. Care for them even after death by making lasting plans. Love outlives death when we allow honesty to guide us. Life after the death of a loved one is so much less painful for the bereaved if that person has made a will. A will is a lasting document of love that honors the truth of death and leaves whatever possessions the deceased had in the hands of loved ones. It is the ultimate act of love to make plans for when you are gone.

You Can't Measure Your Faith, or Anyone Else's for That Matter

The apostles said to the Lord, "Increase our faith!"

The Lord replied, "If you had faith the size of a mustard seed, you could say to this mulberry tree, 'Be uprooted and planted in the sea,' and it would obey you.

LUKE 17:5–6

Why is it that human beings always want more? If we hadn't wanted more, we might not have taken that forbidden fruit in the Garden of Eden. If we hadn't wanted more, we might not have fallen from God. Long after that fatal mistake, we still want more. Just look at the latest advertisements. Our entire American culture is built on the premise that more is better and that better is more. If only we could say when enough is enough. If only we could be satisfied. If only we knew how to be thankful with what God has given us.

The disciples also wanted more. They wanted more faith, but they had no idea what they were asking for. Faith is something you cannot measure. There is no such thing as more faith.

I have a friend whose daughter died of leukemia while he was in seminary. She was five years old. At the time, people would come up to him and say, "Thank God for your faith." Or, they would say, "Just hold on to your faith." He had no idea what they were talking about. Was faith something he was supposed to own or lean on, something that would make this blackness better? If so, he decided he must be missing it. Instead of feeling faith, all he felt was despair.

When the disciples ask for more faith, Jesus gives them a strange answer. If you had faith as tiny as a mustard seed (you know how small those seeds are; they blow away with the wind), you could make a tree jump into the water. You do not know what you are asking. You do not know what faith is.

If faith can make trees jump into the water, it must be powered by God, because only God can do things like that. Nothing a person could create or own or hold on to could make a tree jump into the water. Jesus must have been talking about God when he said that. Faith must be nothing other than God at work in us.

Maybe that's what it is, faith. Maybe faith is, quite simply, the Holy Spirit living inside us—that glimmer of mystery that yearns to return to God, that sliver of hope that nudges us, calls us, presses us to be better people, to seek heaven itself.

My friend who lost his daughter tried to hold on to his faith, but that didn't seem to work for him. After a year of trying, Brad gave up and let the darkness come. He missed his little girl so much. The worst pain came when he thought of the parts of life she would never experience: her first kiss, her prom, her wedding, children. When he thought of all that she was deprived of in death, it seemed as though his despair might swallow him whole.

But when Brad stopped trying so hard to have faith, something else came with the darkness. He had a dream. In the dream, Jesus took his little girl by the hand, and together, they experienced everything. She had her first kiss, got married, and had children; she did *everything*. When he woke up, Brad knew his daughter was alive with God—*really alive*—and experiencing all that is life and love.

This thing called faith cannot be measured. We cannot make it increase or decrease, because it does not come from us. Faith is a gift, a portion of God that lives in us, something completely mysterious and unfathomable. Faith is nothing short of God within us.

Share Your Experience of God with Others

Jesus took with him Peter and James and his brother John and led them up a high mountain, by themselves. And he was transfigured before them, and his face shone like the sun, and his clothes became dazzling white. Suddenly there appeared to them Moses and Elijah, talking with him. Then Peter said to Jesus, "Lord, it is good for us to be here; if you wish, I will make three dwellings here, one for you, one for Moses, and one for Elijah." While he was still speaking, suddenly a bright cloud overshadowed them, and from the cloud a voice said, "This is my Son, the Beloved; with him I am well pleased; listen to him!" When the disciples heard this, they fell to the ground and were overcome by fear. But Jesus came and touched them, saying, "Get up and do not be afraid." And when they looked up, they saw no one except Jesus himself alone.

MATTHEW 17:1–8

Some three hundred years after the resurrection of Jesus, a young man named Paul lived in Thebes. Paul was the son of wealthy parents. He led a life of great comfort until his parents both died when he was just sixteen. Paul was a Christian, and a wave of persecution against Christians had just broken out in Thebes. Paul decided to hide from the violence by living in a cave out in the desert until things calmed down. He discovered that he liked the solitude in that cave, so he stayed.

Legend has it that, one hundred years later, St. Anthony (who would later be known as a great desert mystic) was living his own life of solitude when he heard of an old man who had spent his entire life praying in a cave. Anthony went on a search to find this man, and he found Paul.

As Anthony approached Paul's cave, the old man hobbled out to greet him. Paul looked ancient. Light shone from his eyes. The two men embraced one another without a word. Paul took Anthony's arrival as a sign from God that he was soon to go to heaven. Paul didn't want to scare Anthony, so he asked the young man to fetch him a cloak from the city. Anthony obeyed, leaving Paul alone. But Anthony was quicker than Paul had anticipated. He returned too soon, and this is what he saw: Paul was shining. Anthony would later describe him as a "dazzling, snowy white." He seemed to be speaking to someone, and then he died.

If you look across all the major world religions, you will see the same phenomenon: the holy people who spend their lives in prayer seem to emanate light. There is a reason why Buddhists called the Buddha's state of consciousness *enlightenment.* When he sat under the Bodhi tree, he seemed to shine. In fact, he is often painted with a circle of light around his head. Hindu saints demonstrated the same phenomenon. This is where the concept of a halo or aura comes from. (Though when a masseuse told me she wanted to rub down my aura, I found that a bit much.) So it is no surprise that, when Jesus goes up on a mountain to pray, he begins to shine.

He had probably encountered God in this way many times. This time, though, he had company. Jesus brings his friends with him, and they witness this most intimate moment between him and God. He willingly shares it with them, and they, especially Peter, make a mess of things. (I am convinced that Peter was an extrovert. He processed verbally, and he was always putting his foot in his mouth.) When Peter witnesses this light beyond light, he starts talking, and his words exemplify everything our human minds do when we come closer to God. He is the soul of distraction.

Peter wants to capture the moment, fix the situation, and take control. He thinks of what he can do rather than just being. He rambles on in the midst of great beauty that should have rendered him silent. God has to yell at him from out of the cloud, "This is my Son . . . *Listen to him!*"

Did Jesus know that Peter would interrupt his communion with God? Why did he bring his friends with him anyway? Didn't he know they would not be ready to experience such holiness without getting distracted? Why did Jesus share this kind of intimacy with us? He shared because he loves us and wants us to know what it is to commune with God. Jesus knew that it is better to bring your friends with you, to share God with them, even if it adds chaos. Our faith is something that we are meant to share with others.

Reflection Questions for Chapter 3

1. Who pushes your buttons?
   What do you have to learn from them?

2. How can you grow up? Are there still aspects of your
   childhood that you carry with you?

3. Is it hard for you to share your experience of God with
   others? Why?

CHAPTER 4

Communicate with Others

Third Week in Lent

Look upon Others with Love and Insight

"Martha, Martha, you are worried and distracted by many things; there is need of only one thing. Mary has chosen the better part, which will not be taken away from her."

LUKE 10:41

Jesus saw others clearly and was able to love them, flaws and all. He communicated in a way that helped those around him gain self-understanding.

Jesus visited his friends in Bethany with some frequency. Though the lines between disciples and friends seemed to blur during the course of his ministry (he even called his disciples friends), the family of Bethany did not appear to follow Jesus on his travels. Instead, they were householders who loved Jesus and offered him a place of rest and refuge. In some ways, you could say that Bethany was the closest thing Jesus had to a home.

Martha was busy doing women's work when Jesus came to call that day. She bustled about cleaning and cooking while her sister Mary sat at Jesus' feet as one would sit at the feet of an elder or teacher. Mary's posture showed her adoration and respect for Jesus. It was her way of acknowledging her teacher's insight and wisdom. She sat and listened to him in order to gain understanding. But Martha was angered by her sister's focus. Mary was not helping! The dinner had to be made, and the preparations completed for Jesus to stay as their guest.

Perhaps Martha sighed and threw out all sorts of guilt-trips and hints which Mary, who was absorbed in the love of Jesus, did not catch. Finally, Martha blurted out her frustration to Jesus: "Tell her to help me!"

Instead of voicing her anger directly to Mary, Martha triangulated, bringing in Jesus as a third party. She asked him to take sides and rescue her from her frustration. She saw herself as the harder worker, the misunderstood victim, and she wanted acknowledgment. She wanted to hear them say, "Poor Martha! We have been neglecting you!"

Kitchen wars are common in many families. Who does the cooking? Who does the cleaning? Is it fair? Many marriages are beaten down by the guilt trips and anger of the worker bee who is frustrated with a slower-moving spouse.

Jesus did not let Martha divert the attention from herself. He addressed her directly and identified the anxiety that led to her anger. He told her to slow down, that Mary had it right. "Worship me, and the details will sort themselves out," he seemed to say.

It was as if Jesus could see right into Martha's heart. He said her name twice. I wish I could have heard his tone of voice. I assume that he was fond of her and wanted her to listen to him. Perhaps he spoke slowly, as if to quiet her mind.

What Martha really resented was the peace of mind that Mary achieved. She was jealous of Mary, and Jesus did not try to fix the situation. Rather, he urged her to look to Mary as an example of devotion, to see her as a role model.

I remember arriving all up-in-arms to a church meeting one evening. My husband and my kids had left me a messy house to clean. I voiced my frustration to a woman whose children were grown. She said something so wise I will never forget it: "If you want the house to be clean, clean it. Don't guilt trip anybody else into doing it. If you are the only one who cares about it, then it is your problem and yours alone. Frankly, I think that I'd rather watch my kids grow up than clean a house. You'll be able to keep it clean when they are grown." I felt as if someone had thrown cold water over me. What was I doing, obsessing over such silly things? If I continued in this way, I would miss my kids' childhood!

What did Martha feel when Jesus spoke to her? I imagine that she felt a little like a client who sits down in front of a really intuitive therapist and, in a matter of seconds, hears the therapist hit the nail on the head. I imagine that she felt naked, as if someone had just seen her for the first time. Martha needed to get her priorities straight. She had been focusing on the wrong thing. Why clean the house when Jesus was there? It was crazy!

Jesus confronted Martha, yet he clearly loved her. What a wonderful feeling when a person understands your limitations, but loves you anyway! Sometimes there is really nothing more comforting than being loved, flaws and all.

LENT III: MONDAY

Face Conflict, Face Change

"Do not think that I have come to bring peace to the earth; I have not come to bring peace, but a sword. For I have come to set a man against his father, and a daughter against her mother, and a daughter-in-law against her mother-in-law; and one's foes will be members of one's own household."

MATTHEW 10:34–36

I avoid conflict. I hate it. I will do almost anything to calm someone who is angry. When someone dislikes me, I rack my brain to find the reason why. I will volunteer to do things I cannot follow through on. I will acquiesce to points I don't agree with. I will ignore my children's and my own needs in the name of peace.

Peacemaking is not the same as conflict avoidance. Jesus knew this. He was not afraid of conflict. He knew that his radical new understanding of God was going to threaten people. He knew that his worldview would tear at the very fabric of our belief systems, yet he did not waver. Though he was potently intuitive, he was not willing to compromise the truth just to make people comfortable.

Any change in the church shakes people up. Our church is contemplating a renovation and expansion of our facility. The addition of new walls, new paint, and new fixtures seems to threaten many of the people in the parish. The underlying current, if it were spoken aloud, would go something like this, "Don't you dare change my church. It's fine just the way it is."

Those who express such concerns about change often attribute them to a desire to save money. But money is just a symptom of a deeper issue: people don't want new ideas, and they don't want new buildings. The better things are, the less people are inclined to want change.

Jesus was change incarnate. His message was not nice. It was not easy to hear or understand. It cut to the chase. Bare bones truth can do that.

When the Christian writer, Frederick Buechner, was just a boy, his father committed suicide. He looked in on his boys, then went down to the garage where he purposefully poisoned himself with carbon monoxide. Buechner would later write that it was as if he placed himself in a box that day. He did not want to be hurt again. Though his was not a conscious choice, he began to live from deep inside himself. He described his figurative box as being just big enough to crouch down in, but with no room for movement and certainly no room for growth.

The box kept him safe throughout his childhood. He survived, but was not fully alive. He could not grow or feel. As an adult, when his life did not seem to work, Buechner entered therapy. The process of counseling was terrifying. He felt as if a sword was cutting through his box, pulling away at the walls, and uncovering a vulnerable naked self—a very hurt person who was also (thanks be to God!) alive and capable of joy.

Jesus tears apart the securities we cling to and pulls us out of our darkness into the light. This process can be a violent one. It can tear at the fabric of who we are. It cuts through all our defenses so that we stand naked before God as we once stood in the Garden of Eden. This way of Jesus' is no gentle path. It is life-changing. It is scary. It demands your very soul.

LENT III: TUESDAY

Show Your Feelings

Mary said, "Lord, if you had been here, my brother would not have died."... Jesus began to weep.

JOHN 11:32, 35

Funny, isn't it, that Jesus should try to hide his miracles and yet openly show his emotions? Jesus cried in front of many people, without hiding. He cried openly.

I have this habit of crying when a bride walks down the aisle. There is something so beautiful about that moment. I am constantly tearing up. You would think that, after performing so many weddings, I'd get used to it, but it hits me every time in the gut. It is just so beautiful.

I used to scold myself a lot. I was the priest; I wasn't supposed to cry. I tried every kind of mental exercise to prevent the tears: I pictured the congregation asleep and imagined myself making horrible mistakes. I even tried to think about the errands I needed to run. Nothing worked. The bride would come down the aisle, and I would cry.

Then I really read this verse from Scripture. Jesus cried, too. He wept for the death of his friend. His ministry was not a detached one. He truly cared.

When Jesus wept, he did not try to hide it. He did not do visual exercises or pretend he had allergies. He cried openly and freely, letting the tears flow. Jesus felt pain. His empathy was so great that he felt grief, suffering, and loss. Isn't that the greatest risk of love—that we might end up hurting? Jesus loved greatly, and he felt great pain.

A woman came to me yesterday. "I find myself crying in church," she said. "I'm so sorry. . . . I feel so embarrassed." I reassured her. Church is a great place to cry. Jesus wept. We need to remember that Jesus wept.

Get Mad

Jesus said to them, "Isaiah prophesied rightly about you hypocrites, . . . You abandon the commandment of God and hold to human tradition."

MARK 7:6, 8

When Jesus got angry, he did not try to hide it. He expressed his anger with force and conviction.

The Pharisees and Scribes were devout Jews who devoted their lives to studying and adhering to God's law. You would think they would have asked Jesus to tell them how he prayed or what he believed about God. Instead, they got all caught up in the details of the observance of the law. They became concerned because Jesus performed a miracle on the sabbath. They questioned him about matters of remarriage and divorce. And, in this gospel text, they criticized the disciples who neglected to wash their hands before eating.

Nothing seemed to make Jesus angrier than the petty criticisms of the Pharisees and Scribes. Jesus was harsh and rude to them. They upset him, and he did not mince words when responding to them. He called them snakes and hypocrites. He found more fault with their brand of religious piety than with the practices of those who claimed no religion at all. When he argued with the Pharisees, you would have thought Jesus was fighting the devil himself.

Why was he so adamant, so rude? Why do his words bite, sting, alienate, and confound us, even today? Why did Jesus find it necessary to be so blatantly upsetting?

C. S. Lewis gives us great insight into the nature of evil in his book, *The Screwtape Letters*. In a series of letters between a servant of the devil and his nephew, we see how evil works. If the evil one intends on crippling the good news of Christ, how does he do it? Does he attack Jesus' divinity? Does he claim that Jesus was a criminal or crazy? No, the nature of evil is to work subtly. The evil one does not attack Christ head on; that would lead Christians to come to his defense. Instead, he distracts us, making us think that we must war with each other over matters that are not central to our faith. Should we or shouldn't we wash our hands? What about who can celebrate the Eucharist? The evil one not only provokes us to disagree about these issues, but he also gets us to forget that they are not doctrinal and to forget that what unites us is the love that we bear for Christ.

Jesus said, "You abandon the commandment of God and hold to human tradition." You forget to love your neighbor because you are so obsessed with gender, sexual orientation, and religious practice. The Pharisees had lost their way. Their religious practices no longer focused on God. They had lost God in the midst of the details.

The commandments of God are written in eternity, and they are clear. The Great Commandment of Jesus is "Love the Lord your God with all your heart, and with all your soul, and with all your mind, and with all your strength. . . . And love your neighbor as yourself" (Mark 12:30, 31). The Ten Commandments are also clear: do not steal, do not murder, do not commit adultery, etc.. These are basic laws, which must be upheld to create a civilized human society and to further our love of God and neighbor.

Human tradition is much more nebulous. Like language, it must constantly be reexamined, retranslated, reviewed. It must be evaluated in light of the Great Commandment. For example, the Bible must be translated again and again because language changes. New words are invented and old words acquire new meaning. The same is true of human tradition. Whipping oneself was once considered an act of spiritual devotion. Today we consider it hateful to the human body that God has made. Once a moral man could own a slave. Now we understand that he cannot own a slave and live a life of devotion to God. Once a woman could be owned as a possession. Now we see her as a human being equal to a man. As we grow in understanding, we must translate human tradition in order to remain faithful to the commandments of God.

Why did the Pharisees make Jesus so angry? I think their criticisms infuriated him because they were a sign of wasted human potential. Here were devout men who had supposedly dedicated their lives to God. In reality, though, they had let themselves be tempted by the evil one. They had become shells of devotion, arguing over trivial matters and no longer seeking God's revelation. God Incarnate was before them, yet all they could do was hold fast to their human traditions and criticize those who neglected them. The Pharisees used Scripture as an idol, a barrier to true devotion. Obeying the letter of the law kept them from listening to the living words of Jesus.

It is dangerous to practice Christianity. Doing so requires that we try to discern Christ's will for our lives. It means that we run the risk of becoming distracted and enveloped by obsessions in the name of faith. Around the world our churches are more divided than ever. We have let ourselves become consumed with behavioral practices and gender differences. We have abandoned the commandments of God in order to hold to human tradition, in all denominations. I believe that such behavior makes the living Christ truly angry.

Get Really Mad

The Passover of the Jews was near, and Jesus went up to Jerusalem. In the temple he found people selling cattle, sheep, and doves, and the money changers seated at their tables. Making a whip of cords, he drove all of them out of the temple, both the sheep and the cattle. He also poured out the coins of the money changers and overturned their tables. He told those who were selling the doves, "Take these things out of here! Stop making my Father's house a marketplace!"

JOHN 2:13–16

I had a professor at Yale who loved liturgy. He wanted every worship service to be perfect. If anyone made a mistake in a ceremony, he hit the roof. His class consisted of a constant stream of stories. He would pace the room in a fury, describing the minute details of a service ruined by someone's careless mistake. These small misdemeanors gave him fits.

My professor's anger concerned me at first. I couldn't figure out what the big deal was. Then I realized how deeply he loved God and how vital it was for him that we take time and effort to prepare to worship God. He viewed worship as a sign of our love for God and wanted our expression of that love to be perfect.

When Jesus witnessed people engaged in commerce in the temple, he had a fit. He made a mess. He scared people. I am so thankful that he did this for us, for we often confuse anger with rage. Human beings are prone to think it is wrong to get angry, but the honest and healthy person gets angry. If you care about what you are doing, you will get mad. And it is good to know that Jesus got mad, too.

Jesus was violent as well. He made a whip, and he chased people out of the temple complex. He acted on his anger. Most of us don't act on our anger for fear that we might make a scene, disrupt the status quo, or make a mess. In avoiding the expression of our anger, we make our popularity more important than our honesty. Conflict can be holy. Conflict is not bad; it is an agent of change.

I spoke with a mom at church who said this idea changed the way she was raising her kids. At first, she hid her anger all the time. No matter what they did, she tried to remain calm and cool because she didn't want to traumatize them with her anger. But she began to realize that her children were running right over her and growing up with no consideration for how she felt or what she thought. So she changed. Now, when something makes her mad, she gets mad. She even yells sometimes. She shows them how upset she is. Then, when her anger has dissipated, they talk about what made her mad. In this way, her kids are learning how to express their own anger. And they are learning that their mom has feelings, too.

Making sure no one is upset is not the Christian way. Followers of Jesus must admit that Jesus not only endured conflict, he created it. He expressed his displeasure. He got really angry.

Standing up for what is right is hard to do. It is uncomfortable. It is disturbing. But the alternative is pretending that everything is okay when it is not. The alternative is dishonesty, even idolatry. That is why we must have the courage to be openly angry. Justified anger is sometimes the only way to tell the truth in this broken world.

See the Brokenness

But when I looked for good, evil came;
and when I waited for light, darkness came.

JOB 30:26

I sit in the office of my spiritual director. It took me years to find her. She is a Quaker with a Ph.D. in spiritual direction, and she is good. I tell her about the darkness that I see, about how people can't stand speaking about money, about the ways they hurt one another and actively undermine efforts to grow the church. I tell her about the brokenness.

"That is what you are supposed to see now," she says. "When one begins to really pray, when the time one spends alone with God begins to shape your life, one of the first things that happens is that you open your eyes to the brokenness of the world around you. You see that we have fallen from God, and that it is hard to avoid sin."

We feel helpless when we face evil and its consequences. The suffering and brokenness of the world loom large. Such an overpowering sense of the negative can cause Christians to stop regarding the surrounding world. I asked a New Yorker who had lived in Manhattan all her life how she copes with the homeless who are all around her on the streets. She said, "Well, to be honest with you, I just don't see them anymore."

I think that Jesus looked at the devil, spoke with the devil, and rejected the devil *all on our behalf.* He modeled for us what it means to be healthy—to listen and look at the darkness and reject it.

The devil, that adversary who would have us distance ourselves from God, wants to hide from us as well. Secrecy and avoidance are his bread and butter. If you want to serve God, you must bring light into the darkness. You must shine a flashlight into the dusty closet of your past and see your own brokenness as well as the brokenness of those around you. Only when we see ourselves in this way can we begin to hope and pray for salvation. In fact, salvation means nothing without the notion that we are estranged from God. If we don't believe we need saving, why cry out to the Savior?

LENT III: SATURDAY

God Is Here, . . . Now!

And Jesus would say, "The kingdom of God has come near!"

MARK 1:15

Jesus constantly tried to communicate with people about what he called *the kingdom of God,* or *the kingdom of heaven.* When Jesus spoke about the kingdom of God, he spoke of it as immediate, not some aspect of the afterlife or of heaven as we define it today, but a reality that is present here and now. Jesus also spoke of being awake. Could it be that *the realm of God* (another way to render the kingdom of God) is right around us? Could it be that God is present, but we are blind to that presence?

We know that there is much we cannot see. Both the microscopic and the macroscopic worlds remain imperceptible to us, though their existence has been confirmed. There are many more dimensions than the three we've been taught to recognize. What if Jesus could see and sense more than we can? What if Jesus could perceive the immediate presence of God?

For Jesus, it must have been kind of like the time I came home from the airport. I missed my two-year-old son, Max, so much. When I reached the house, the door was already open.

My husband, JD, stood in the living room. His face lit up when I stepped inside, but Max had his back to me. JD could see that I was home, and he knew that Max had been waiting for me, but Max had not yet seen me. We shared a moment of sweetness as we waited for Max to turn around.

"Repent," Jesus said. "Turn around." Can't you see that God is immediately present with you? Open your eyes. Your love has walked through the door and is smiling, waiting for your eyes to open.

Reflection Questions for Chapter 4

1. Are you able to share your emotions with others?
   Why or why not?

2. Who makes you mad?
   Can you express that anger in a positive way?

3. Describe a complex relationship in your life. How can you
   look upon this person with both love and insight?

CHAPTER 5

Form Godly Habits

Fourth Week in Lent

Eat

"I am the bread of life. Whoever comes to me will never be hungry, and whoever believes in me will never be thirsty."

JOHN 6:35

Today, when we are hungry, we stop by a drive-through. We no longer know what true hunger feels like—the kind that leaves you feeling like you're going to die or like your stomach may claw itself apart. Jesus' disciples knew hunger. Since they fished for their food, a good catch meant a good meal. A day of no fish meant a day without food. No wonder the biblical vision of heaven was of a table covered with food. For people of biblical times, there was no greater sign of continued life than a table heavy with meat, fish, and produce. Life eternal was a place with *a lot* of food.

Eating is still just as central to our existence, but we have forgotten its significance because our needs are always met. How many times have I wolfed down a burrito without so much as a nod to God for providing me with a delicious meal-on-the-run? Sometimes I can't even remember what I have eaten that day; it has become that effortless to nourish my body. If I were deprived of food for even one day, I would remember its importance.

Eating is so central to our existence that humanity fell from God's grace in and through the act of eating. If we had not consumed that which was not offered, if we had not taken the fruit of the Tree of the Knowledge of Good and Evil, we would not be so lost. Our world fell out of harmony with God because we ate something that was not freely given to us by God.

Jesus offers the antidote to our fall from grace. There is really only one way to convince his followers of salvation. He must feed us with the food of eternal life. He must give of himself, and let us all consume his flesh. The key to eternity is in the eating.

Could Jesus have just explained God's love to us? Would it have worked to explain the extravagance of God's love? No. We could never grasp this kind of love intellectually. The only way Jesus can convince us of that kind of love is to let us consume it. After all, that is what we human beings do. We consume. A baby's first motion when it learns to pick up an object is to put that object in its mouth. Babies test the world by tasting it. Our deepest, most infantile selves fear oblivion. So God lets us taste salvation.

The act of offering his flesh also leaves room for us to refuse. Jesus does not force-feed us. We are simply invited. For all eternity, the invitation is open. Come, he says, taste and see the goodness of the Lord. Or, as George Herbert, the Anglican priest and poet, wrote centuries ago:

"You must sit down," says Love, "And taste my meat."
So I did sit, and eat.

The Eucharist is just that, the meat of love. Once we catch a glimpse of the incredible nature of this gift that is given to us in bread and wine, we cannot stop thanking God. No response—no words, or gifts, or money, or time—is enough to thank God for the gift that Jesus gives us, the gift of eternity.

Talk About Money

"Blessed are you who are poor, for yours is the kingdom of God."

LUKE 6:20

Jesus continually spoke about money. The topic of money, which is today so fraught with complication and taboo, was a frequent topic of Jesus' teachings. He wanted to tell us that our relationship with money plays a role in our devotional lives.

I once stood on the Mount of the Beatitudes, the place where it is believed that Jesus said these words. The wind blew off the Sea of Galilee. It was beautiful. To think that such a place of natural beauty was once witness to some of the most complex words in all of history! Scholars have been trying to grapple with Jesus' beatitudes ever since the resurrection. Could he actually have meant that the poor are favored by God? Is it wrong to be rich? Many saints and sinners have sold all that they have in the attempt to live out these words. Others have tried to ignore or weaken the same words.

Why would Jesus condemn the wealthy ("Woe to you who are rich" Luke 6:24a)? What is it about money that distances us from God? Is there a way to be wealthy and saintly? Do we really have to choose between our money and God? One possibility I cannot deny is that Jesus was speaking a stark, literal truth, namely, that money is full of sin. Those who love God must prove their love by shedding their wealth, as Jesus suggested to the rich man. This interpretation is unacceptable for most Americans because we are unwilling to give up our privilege. So, we are bound and determined to seek an interpretation that will not challenge our standard of living.

New stewardship ministries are arising all over the church. Talking openly about money is now encouraged, but the majority of Americans would still rather discuss their abdominal surgeries than divulge their income. Why is money such tricky stuff, and why did Jesus say that it was better not to have it?

Jesus talked about money more than he spoke about prayer. There is no denying that he considered our monetary life to be as important as our prayer life. We cannot divorce our devotion from our dollars; one is an expression of the other. Even so, did he really mean to condemn those of us who are unwilling to sell everything? Surely he didn't mean to condemn us, did he?

Years ago, I visited a woman in a detox unit. She was addicted to narcotics and was drying out. She described her recovery in terms I had never heard before. She spoke of being alone in a dark room, sweating and shaking. No one was there for her. She was totally alone, and she contemplated death. Then something, or Someone, happened. A presence of love and strength, such as she had never felt before, entered her heart. For the first time in her life, she sensed the presence of God.

Why did it take hitting rock bottom for God to enter her heart? I believe that there was no room inside her soul until the moment came when she recognized her poverty. Once she realized her emptiness, God could fill it. There was space for God to enter. Blessed was the emptiness. Blessed was her poverty, her solitary room, her loneliness. She was blessed by hitting rock bottom and realizing that Someone was there with her.

Blessed are the poor, for they need God. If we truly think that anything else can comfort us and love us as God can, then we are suffering from a terrible delusion. God alone can fill our hearts. Blessed is the emptiness when we invite God to fill it.

We must give of our resources generously, not just to do God's work, but to free ourselves from the illusion that our money is ours and ours alone. Our money belongs to God. Once we realize that incredible truth and recognize our own poverty, we can begin to do great good.

LENT IV: TUESDAY

Give Money Away

"Give, and it will be given to you. A good measure, pressed down, shaken together, running over, will be put into your lap; for the measure you give will be the measure you get back."

LUKE 6:38

The discipline of giving is not an option in the life of Christian; it is essential. Jesus was very clear on the subject of giving. We must give. Giving tempers our selfish nature and fills us with joy. When we give, it is as if we are handing the forbidden fruit back to God. Who said that it was ours anyway? It was never ours. It was God's, from the very beginning, now and forever.

Jesus promises great rewards for giving. I can say that these rewards are real. I see them every day. The people in my congregation who give generously are happier. The ones who complain the most generally give the least. Those who give find themselves healthier psychologically and emotionally. They experience great joy in life.

It is hard to talk about money and giving. I find myself caught up in fund-raising and forget that my business is really

God-raising. I am about trying to help people come closer to Jesus, and if that means talking about money, so be it.

Jesus didn't seem to mind making people uncomfortable. He didn't seem to have self-doubt. He didn't anxiously await a reaction. He just told the truth. He walked right into the most difficult of conversations and spoke clearly, without hesitation. Give and it will be given to you. Is there anything else that needs to be said? If you want to be unhappy, cling to your life: your belongings, your money, your relationships. If you want to be well, then be generous. Give it all away, serve God and not yourself. And God, who alone knows how to make you happy, will do just that.

Stay Private About Your Generosity

"Whenever you give alms, do not sound a trumpet before you, as the hypocrites do in the synagogues and in the streets, so that they may be praised by others. . . . But when you give alms, do not let your left hand know what your right hand is doing, so that your alms may be done in secret; and your Father who sees in secret will reward you."

MATTHEW 6:2a, 3–4

Jesus was not a people-pleaser. He did not utter words with the intention of angering or pleasing others. He spoke truth. His constant guide was God alone. What would God want? What was God asking of him? Though he was incredibly intuitive and able to understand the minds of others, Jesus did not seem to be swayed by their opinions.

Our American culture today thrives on people-pleasing. Capitalism is completely dependent on consumerism, and people will not buy what they do not like. Therefore, what pleases people becomes successful, earns money, and makes jobs. Pleasing people means survival in the business world. If you want to survive, you must learn to please.

Our people-pleasing has led us to become innately geared toward popular opinion. We do feasibility studies. We take votes. What is most popular must be right, the logic goes. The entire premise of democracy (and believe me when I say that I believe there is no better form of government) is approval. One cannot be elected to lead this country without pleasing more people than the other guy. People-pleasing is leadership. It is survival. It is essential.

Jesus did not seek to please. He did not seem to bear the insecurities that come with a life of striving to make others happy. He knew that any devotional act, if done in public, was in danger of being reduced to showing off. So he told us to pray in private. Why not tell others how much money you donated? Because it muddies the waters. As you feel the pride and even justifiable joy that comes with generosity, you become subject to distraction. You forget that it was because of God, and no one else, that you gave.

Keeping secrets can hurt others. On the other hand, keeping secrets for God gives life. Keeping a secret for God—a secret that is really only between you and God anyway—ratchets up your fidelity to God. Essentially, you and God begin to have a private love affair. No other kind of love affair is as faithful and enhances as many other human relationships as a love affair with God.

This kind of quiet giving that Jesus speaks of is not easy. Conducting this private love affair with God will require plenty of self-discipline. Because time given to God in prayer yields abundant blessings, you may feel like shouting from the rooftops that you just spent an hour in prayer. Because generous living begets even more generosity, you may be tempted to reveal how much money you give, in the hopes that someone will be inspired, challenged, and moved to follow your example. Take care that you do not give away your secret. Remember, God already knows and is already filling you with blessings.

Remember That the Body Is the Home of the Soul

Jesus ordered them to tell no one; but the more he ordered them, the more zealously they proclaimed it.

MARK 7:36

Why did Jesus not want people to talk about his miracles? Why did he not want the news of his healing work to spread? He was adamant when he told his disciples that he wanted them to spread the news of the kingdom. "Tell them that the kingdom of God is near," he would instruct them. Yet, miracles of healing, he did not want discussed. The disciples must have found this secrecy puzzling.

Jesus performed numerous miracles, but the needs of humanity were much greater than what his two hands could touch. I do not believe that he performed miracles because he favored those whom he healed. I believe that he performed miracles as the means to a message, a message that was far more important than the health of a person's physical body. Isaiah foretold that the Messiah would heal—the lame would walk and the blind would see (Isaiah 35:5–6). That is what the prophet foretold. Jesus must have known that if people were to listen to his message at all that he would have to heal. His healing opened their minds to the possibility of his messiahship. Because of the miracles, people listened.

But Jesus' miracles were not the last word. They were not his main message. He came to us to give us something far greater. For Jesus, healing the physical body was like putting a band-aid on a serious wound. It was like fixing the engine of an old car so that it will run awhile longer. The physical body was not his focus. He wanted to tell us about something more.

The boy who lives next door to us has been fighting cancer for four years. He has to wear hearing aids to school because his treatment is so radical that he has lost some of his hearing. Why does God not heal him? Does God not love this wonderful little boy as much as God loved the deaf man, the blind man, and the paralytic?

Many faith and healing groups cry out to God for miracles. I do, too. I hold a healing service once a week. We unabashedly ask God for health in the midst of sickness. Sometimes miracles happen, but other times people die. I believe that Jesus loves the sick and the dying just as much as he loves those who are healthy.

Yet for God, the most important thing is not the health of the body, but the health of the soul. Jesus was trying to announce a gift that he was giving to all humanity, the gift of eternal life. A perfect body waits for us in heaven. This body in heaven is like our physical one here, but it is more fully ours, more perfectly harmonious with who we are. In our baptism, that life eternal is gifted to us. That is the greatest miracle.

I believe that we should care for our physical bodies, but with the awareness that there is much more that exists in God. God adores you even if you fall ill.

LENT IV: FRIDAY

Being Late Can Be a Holy Thing

Though Jesus loved Martha and her sister and Lazarus, after having heard that Lazarus was ill, he stayed two days longer in the place where he was.

JOHN 11:5–6

I find it fascinating that Jesus was late when one of his friends was dying. In a very serious matter, he was late. His friend Lazarus was dying, and Jesus waited two days to travel to him. Two days! By the time Jesus arrived, Lazarus was dead.

Some scholars surmise that Jesus intended to be late so that he could bring Lazarus back from the dead. I find this kind of calculated set-up for a miracle to be quite unlike Jesus. As far as I know, at no other time does he stage a miracle, so I assume that he did not do that here. He was just late. He thought that he could make it, but he didn't. Upon his arrival, he wept. He wept tears of sadness at the death of his friend and perhaps tears of regret at his own miscalculation.

Timing is tough. I try to get to the bedside the moment that I hear that a parishioner is dying, or as soon as possible. If I can't go, I try to have someone else go by and say prayers, say good-bye. But most of the time, I miscalculate. Death is so much like birth that it is completely unpredictable. One man who was reportedly taking his last breath woke up when I began the prayers and asked what we were doing. The Last Rites stimulated his brain, and his curiosity seemed to revive him. Furthermore, he was annoyed. He wasn't dying! What were we thinking? On the way out, his wife said that she never knew that Last Rites could be so reviving.

I tend to believe that Jesus just didn't get there on time. No doubt he was doing some other vital ministry that kept him from leaving the moment that he heard the news. I feel comforted that even the Son of God was late at least once in his life. Maybe timeliness is not necessarily the same thing as godliness. The important thing is that we are present with the person who is in front of us. Present and awake to listen and to love. In our age of rush-and-schedule devotion, remind yourself that Jesus was late. Sometimes tardiness can be the occasion for a miracle.

It's Okay to Be Lonely

*"Foxes have holes, and birds of the air have nests;
but the Son of Man has nowhere to lay his head."*

MATTHEW 8:20 // LUKE 9:58

Despite the crowds that followed him, despite the close relationships that surrounded him, Jesus did not feel as if he had a home. Jesus felt homeless. That fact is beyond my comprehension. During the last years of his life, he was unable to have a home, a place to rest.

I love my house. Cleaning it relaxes me. I love pulling weeds from the garden and listening to my children play in the front yard. There is a deep sense of belonging that comes from having a home. I feel sad for Jesus, that he was not able to have this kind of rest at the end of his life.

What was it about Jesus that made him homeless? I believe that it was the urgency of his message that forced him to move constantly, spreading the news as best he could. He seemed to know that his time was limited. He seemed to understand that his home was in God and God alone.

He seemed to visit his friends Mary, Martha, and Lazarus with some frequency. Maybe their house was as close to home as he could get. He must have felt lonely when he had to leave his friends in Bethany.

Traveling leaves me exhausted and homesick. Jesus must have grown weary of traveling, too. He must have wanted that warmth, that peace that surrounds a family. He must have hungered for warm food, a clean place to sleep, and someone to greet in the morning. He must have ached when he left his friends to go off on another walking tour. He must have grown tired of sleeping in a new place every night.

The earliest human beings were also nomadic. Unable to generate enough food in one place, they moved about as they needed. Abraham, Jacob, Moses were all travelers. It seems that devotion to God often makes us get up and move.

I wish that I could give Jesus a place to rest in my house. Maybe that's why he did not have a home, so that all of us could invite him into ours and hope that he will one day come inside.

Reflection Questions for Chapter 5

1. Why are we so uncomfortable talking about money? How can you begin to talk about it?

2. What prevents you from giving more generously?

3. How do we make our bodies more important than our souls? What is your highest priority? How much time do you spend worrying about your body, and how much time do you spend preparing your soul?

CHAPTER 6

Live in Community

Fifth Week in Lent

Find a Community

*Then Jesus summoned his twelve disciples and gave them author-
ity over unclean spirits, to cast them out, and to cure every disease and every sickness.*

MATTHEW 10:1

Jesus created portable community. We do not really know why
he chose the twelve men (and some women, too) who became
his closest confidants. Maybe they chose him through their
willingness to drop their lives and follow him. We do know
that they followed him almost everywhere he went.

Churches all over the nation have awakened to the power
of small, portable communities. People who come to church
and find themselves welcomed into a small group that genu-
inely accepts them will almost always come back to that
church. Alcoholics Anonymous is built on the healing power
of such small groups. Many in recovery know of no greater in-
strument for mental healing and support.

It was not uncommon for a religious teacher or prophet in
Jesus' day to have disciples or followers, but Jesus' disciples
played a more constant role in his life than was typical. They

accompanied him on his travels and supported him in his ministry. They provided financial support, fished for food, and cared for the other worldly things Jesus needed in order to survive. Most of all, Jesus' disciples learned from their master.

If Christianity is a process of modeling our lives after Jesus' life, it seems that Christians ought to engage in small-group communities. Corporate worship and time alone with God are important for nurturing faith, but so is experiencing the kind of intimacy that develops in a community of twelve or so people. Small groups can be at the heart of some of our most powerful devotional experiences. Some of the finest wisdom may come to us in the small-group setting. Yet, of the three forms of worship in the Christian life, participation in a small group is seldom considered to be as essential to faith as Sunday morning worship or personal prayer time.

If you truly want to follow Jesus, you must find yourself a group of bumbling, fallible friends. Put yourself in a group of imperfect human beings whose only commonality is a willingness to stick it out together for a period of time. Then, open your life and your heart to them, and watch as you become a better person. The small group is an essential aspect of Jesus' ministry. He chose to spend his final years with twelve people, teaching and devoting himself to them. Who could have known that his teachings would reach to the ends of the earth? And it all started with twelve.

Get Feedback

> *When Jesus came into the district of Caesarea Philippi, he asked*
> *his disciples, "Who do people say that the Son of Man is?" And*
> *they said, "Some say John the Baptist, but others Elijah, and*
> *still others Jeremiah or one of the prophets." He said to them,*
> *"But who do you say that I am?"*

MATTHEW 16:13–15

We clergy are told that we are people-pleasers. Most of us are.
We can't stand it when others are mad at us. We want to know
how we are doing and what the attendance is at church. When
someone seems angry, it drives us crazy. I have taken part in
enough support groups to believe it is true; the majority of
clergy want people to like them. The antidote to people-
pleasing, we are told again and again, is to let go of the expec-
tations of others. Don't live your life to please others; it will
make you miserable. Good advice, though not if taken to the
extreme.

It is important to ask others for feedback in order to understand how effectively we are functioning and how clearly
we are communicating. As human beings, we do not have a

complete picture of ourselves. We must get the opinions of those around us if we are to be of service in the world. We must also have the freedom *not to have to do* that which pleases others.

I once worked with a man who was afraid to ask how he was doing. Numb from staying at the same unrewarding job for years, he did not seek to find out whether or not he was reaching people. He ran from the opinions of others and gave off an air of nonchalance and boredom. Deep inside, though, he felt ineffective and lonely.

For clergy to ask their congregations to give them an evaluation is risky. One consultant advised me to get a group of trusted laity together and ask them, "How am I doing?" Let them give feedback, both the positive and, perhaps more importantly, the negative. This practice has helped me a lot, though my stomach does a back flip every time I meet with the group.

Feedback is important because it helps us separate fact from fiction. My parishioners may actually be bored when I think that they are angry. When I am speaking, they may be thinking of something besides what they are hearing. It is helpful to take to heart this truth about ourselves and others: we spend very little time thinking of anything else but our own experience.

Jesus was not afraid to ask how he was doing. He was careful to ask this question of people who loved him, people who were committed to his ministry, people he could trust. But he did dare to ask. Midway through his ministry, he stops to get an evaluation. And when Peter names him the Messiah, when Peter gets the message, Jesus begins his journey to the cross.

It is amazing that the Son of God asked others what they thought. He had to, because, no matter how incredible he was, he could not tell what was going on in the minds of others until he asked them. Honest human communication begins with the courage to ask a question of another and then to listen for the answer.

Give Up on First Place

"So the last will be first, and the first will be last."

MATTHEW 20:16

Human beings are genetically competitive. We want to be the best. We teach our children to win at sports. We quiz them about who in their class is the best speller. We compare how fast our babies are developing. Last month two parents got into a screaming match on a basketball court, and over what? A first-grade foul shot.

The religious conflict that embroils our world is, at its roots, about nothing more than whom God favors. Who are the chosen people of God? The Jews? The Muslims? The Christians? Whom does God love the most?

On the road to Capernaum, the disciples got into an argument about who was the greatest. Jesus overheard them, but they didn't know it. When they arrived in town, Jesus sat the disciples down and asked them, "What were you talking about?" They did not answer.

I can just see them squirming in their seats, pretending that they didn't know what he was talking about, getting red in the face, or looking at the floor. The disciples were behaving like kids, but Jesus didn't get mad. He realized that their competitiveness was simply part of who they were as human beings, part of their genetic make-up. So, instead of getting mad, he gave them a vital piece of information about God. With God, you have to be willing to be last. You must take your own status off center stage. You must be willing to be a servant.

What would the world look like if we were really able to do this? What if we gave our land to someone else? What if we stopped teaching our children that they needed to be the best at something? What if we gave up on being first? I wonder how many wars could be averted, how many tragedies prevented?

A Muslim man was brought before Mahatma Gandhi. The man's son had been murdered by a Hindu. He was full of rage and revenge. Gandhi told him not to kill but, instead, to adopt a Hindu child and raise that child as a Hindu. When a Hindu man whose son was killed by a Muslim came to Gandhi, he told him to adopt a Muslim child and raise him as a Muslim.

This kind of forgiveness, this kind of servanthood is almost unheard of. It is so radical that it could only come from Christ. If we could be like him, placing ourselves last, the world would be radically altered for the better.

Don't Gossip

More than ever the word about Jesus spread abroad; many crowds would gather to hear him and to be cured of their diseases. But Jesus would withdraw to deserted places and pray.

LUKE 5:15–16

Jesus rarely talked about anyone. He was almost always engaged in direct discourse. Occasionally he taught the disciples a lesson based on an incident they witnessed, but nowhere in the Gospels does he tell someone about an uninvolved third party. He does not triangulate. It just doesn't seem to be part of his equation.

This kind of direct discourse is difficult to contemplate, let alone practice. It eliminates many of the kinds of discussions we like to have. It limits our options when visiting with others. Imagine if you had to go on a first date and you were mandated not to talk about anyone else. You would be forced to talk solely about yourselves, forcing you into a kind of intimacy which would either end up in love or total disinterest. There would be no safe cushion of gossip to fill in the gaps.

Jesus did have strong feelings about people, but he always expressed those opinions with brutal honesty directly to the person who merited them. He did not report, judge, or criticize people behind their backs. Never.

No wonder he found that he was lonely. What do we have to talk about besides the misfortunes or successes of others? Discussion about a third party, though fascinating, is destructive to those who do the talking. Venting our opinions to a third party when we would never dare to speak to the first party is a form of dishonesty. It is harmful to all three parties involved.

We all know what it feels like to be disliked from afar, to know that someone is gossiping about us. We all know the pain of junior high, when a peer is found spreading rumors about us or insulting us behind our backs. It hurts. It is ugly.

Being directly angry or disappointed takes courage that many of us lack. We are too frightened to risk the displeasure of the one who has offended us, so we vent our negative feelings, displacing them by handing them to a third party, who often hands them off again. The result is gossip and a breakdown of community.

Just yesterday I was complaining about a conference I was attending. "What do you think of it so far?" a stranger asked me on the bus back home. I started to complain about how it wasn't interesting to me, about how the hotel was too expensive, and how the people seemed cliquish. I noticed that the woman across the aisle seemed to be listening in on our conversation so I spoke up a bit. As we were getting off the bus, someone introduced her to me. She was the executive director who had spent an entire year planning the conference. I was mortified. She had worked so hard, and I was mouthing off, spouting criticisms. Was it that I wanted to please her? My judgments were not lies, and yet they sounded too harsh for the person who executed the conference. If I had to report to her directly, I would have cushioned my comments with a few compliments. The food, after all, was excellent.

Speaking directly to others leaves you with one harsh choice to make: Will you be honest about your feelings, or will you hide them for fear of displeasing? We are free to hand out compliments by the dozen, but when it comes to negative impressions, it seems that Jesus was one of a much smaller minority, those who have the courage to tell the truth.

Celebrate with Friends

On the third day there was a wedding in Cana of Galilee, and the mother of Jesus was there. Jesus and his disciples had also been invited to the wedding.

JOHN 2:1–2

Despite the fact that Jesus had nowhere to call home, he still found time to have fun with his friends. Jesus enjoyed a good party. I love that fact. He was there when they drank up the wine! He stayed way beyond the marriage vows. He must have been enjoying himself.

Through the centuries, church has become the opposite of a good party. People go to bars on Saturday night and then say they have to go to church to confess their sins. When someone goes to a crazy party over the weekend, and I ask them how their weekend was, I often get a red-faced stammer for a response.

Drinking and partying have become so synonymous with irresponsibility that many Christians shun liquor entirely. Rumors flew after I carried around a can of beer at a church fair. I was new to the small town and didn't realize the stunning ramifications of a pastor imbibing in public. Since I hardly ever drink, I thought nothing of taking a few sips. That day I became known as "the pastor who drinks beer!"

At a wedding in Jesus' day, people stayed put. Guests would sleep over. There was no danger of drinking and driving. People set aside days to enjoy a party. It was considered an important part of life: resting, enjoying one another's company, celebrating love and the joining together of two people in marriage. Drinking can be dangerous; many people should never take a drink. But we need not forget how to enjoy a good party. Part of our human calling is to celebrate life itself. We can relax, dance, laugh, and rest. Jesus did.

It is not sinful to enjoy yourself. The person who presides over the Holy Eucharist is called *the celebrant*. This person is *the one who celebrates*. After all, when we realize what God has done for us in Jesus, we should want to party well into the night.

Forgive

"Father, forgive them; for they do not know what they are doing."

LUKE 23:34

Jesus told us to forgive others. Over and over and over again, we must forgive. For many Christians there is nothing more difficult than carrying out this mandate. When we get hurt, the typical human urge is to fight back, thus summoning anger, resentment, and rage. After fighting back, we tend to shore up, hide ourselves away, and try to heal. We usually reject the one who wronged us, as if to pretend that what was a hurtful and perhaps violent exchange never happened. Wounds change lives, but we must decide how we want our lives to be changed. Will we hold on to injustice and cling to the role of the victim, or will we let go of our anger and use our wounds as a source of ministry?

The process of forgiveness was instantaneous for Jesus. For us, it can take a lifetime. I knew a woman who was raped repeatedly as a child. It took her fifteen years before she was able to forgive. She testified in court. She went into deep and regular therapy, and she began to live again. And then she found her calling. She ended up a counselor of abused women. She literally took her deepest wound and used it to help others.

The New Testament Greek word for forgiving means *letting go*. Letting go does not mean condoning; that distinction is vital. No one, least of all Jesus, would want a victim to condone the horror that he or she has suffered. Forgiveness is something else entirely. Forgiveness is the letting go you experience when you decide that you will move again, grow again, live again, and love again. You know that you must put down the weight of resentment in order to live, and so you *let it go*.

When you are well enough, you will revisit that wound and take it up again. You will take it up as a cross, put it on, and use it to save lives. What was the cause of death and pain will become a source of new life. That is forgiveness. It is nothing more than resurrection itself.

LENT V: SATURDAY

Friendship

"I do not call you servants any longer, . . . but friends."

JOHN 15:15

Jesus relied on his friends. He seemed to enjoy their support, their questions, their presence. When the disciples left him at the Garden of Gethsemane, Jesus grew quieter. Their desertion of him must have been one of the most painful parts of his life. Thank God that the women remained.

I believe that we were created not because God needs us, but because our presence gives God joy. It was so with Jesus. As much as the disciples exhausted him with their carelessness, ignorance and questions, he did love them. He wanted to be with them. They were his friends.

We can approach God as a friend, as simply someone to talk to. Life is not meant to be lived alone. Human beings are meant to live in community, to be supported by fellowship, to teach one another, and even, at times, to be disappointed by one another. Friendship is an essential aspect of our lives.

Reflection Questions for Chapter 6

1. Do you have a community?
   Can you form one for yourself if you do not?

2. Who are your friends?
   Do they know how important they are in your life?

3. Whom do you need to forgive?

CHAPTER 7

Hold On

Holy Week

Hold Each Other

"O Jerusalem, Jerusalem, the city that kills the prophets and stones those who are sent to it! How often have I desired to gather your children together as a hen gathers her brood under her wings, and you were not willing!"

LUKE 13:34

I have determined that sin is viral. It seems to adapt itself to new circumstances. With all the advances that humanity has made, it seems that we cannot avoid sin. When we make great strides in medical technology, enabling us to cure diseases and alleviate pain, we also end up prolonging death and increasing addiction. No matter how much we learn, the distraction of sin accompanies us. We cannot avoid the alternative to goodness; it is part of who we are.

Things have not changed much in Jerusalem since Jesus' time. Entire cultures are still at war with one another. A young Palestinian girl gets berated and searched at a checkpoint every day on her way to school. Her Christian family, like so many others, is going to leave Israel. The Palestinian Christians are becoming extinct.

Jesus' response to human sin is counter-intuitive. He does not want to punish or correct. He does not try to explain to us what we are doing wrong or how we have gone astray. Instead he wants to embrace us. When my child disobeys me, my first instinct is to punish or at least lecture. I want to explain exactly what he did wrong and why it makes me mad. Jesus does not seem to have the same need to correct. As he sits over Jerusalem, he wants simply to hold us, as a mother would gather a child into her lap to wipe away tears after an injury. When my baby first awakens, he likes to cuddle. Barely aware of his surroundings, he relaxes in my arms, and I rock him. Nothing makes him happier than some early-morning cuddling. It makes for a great day.

Maybe the Son of God does not want to fix us. Maybe he knows that we are too entangled in our confusion to be made perfect in this life. But he does want to hold us. He wants to embrace us. Perhaps the healing power of that kind of unconditional love is a much more potent corrective force.

A teenage boy recently came to a youth retreat at our church. With tattoos and piercings a-plenty, he was a sight to behold. And he was angry. At the retreat, the other kids loved him. They opened his heart with hugs, music, lack of sleep, and laughter. When I saw him at the end of the weekend, his face was shining. He came up to me and shocked me with a huge smile and a hug. How could I think for one moment that some kind of disciplinary action would have been more effective? All he needed was to be loved, to be held.

If only we could allow ourselves to be held by Christ as he yearned to do so long ago. If only we could slow ourselves down and recognize when his arms close in around us.

Let the Grieving Talk About Their Grief

As Jesus approached the gate of the town, a man who had died was being carried out. He was his mother's only son, and she was a widow; and with her was a large crowd from the town. When the Lord saw her, he had compassion for her and said to her, "Do not weep." Then he came forward and touched the bier, and the bearers stood still. And he said, "Young man, I say to you, rise!" The dead man sat up and began to speak, and Jesus gave him to his mother. Fear seized all of them; and they glorified God.

LUKE 7:12–16a

The widow from the village of Nain was in trouble. In those days, women were viewed as possessions rather than as individual people. Women, like cattle or sheep, were owned by their husband. When a woman's husband died, it was understood that her male offspring would care for her. But in today's story, the widow's only son died, leaving her totally alone. She could find herself homeless. She could starve. She was lost.

Almost immediately upon death, a person's body would be wrapped in a cloth, placed on a palate of sorts, and carried to the outskirts of the town to the tombs to be buried. This burial procession had to happen quickly, for the body would decay rapidly in the heat of Israel as there was no procedure for bodily preservation. So the widow found herself parading through the town of Nain weeping.

The gospel says that there was a large crowd accompanying the body. People had probably come along for a variety of reasons. Some just wanted to see what all the excitement was about. Some wanted to gossip about the poor woman: what would she do now? Perhaps some came because they knew her and loved her or loved her son. Maybe some were crying, too.

In the time of Jesus, people grieved more openly. They would scream, wail, and rub dirt on their faces. They expressed feelings of desperation and despair. Grief was chaotic, not like our calm funerals today. It was also honest. We know that the woman from Nain was crying because, when Jesus sees her, the first thing he says is "Don't weep."

One line in this story tells us so much about how Jesus felt about death. *He had compassion for her.* Jesus did not feel sorry for the young man. He was not sad that the man's life had been cut short by death. He was not concerned for the young man's well-being. For Jesus, death was neither scary nor noteworthy. It was the part of life where the soul is embraced by God. No, Jesus did not concern himself with the dead man. He concerned himself with her, the mother. He had compassion for the one who was left alone.

It is not death that saddens God, but loneliness. God does not want us to be alone. Jesus raised the young man from the dead not to rescue him, but to give his mother back her connection to humanity. I used to think that the holiest Christian life was a life spent in isolation. I thought of the monk or the hermit who would retreat into a cave and pray alone for the rest of his life. I thought that this kind of loneliness was ideal devotion, but I was wrong. Jesus did not want that woman to be alone, and I don't believe that God wants us to be alone. Look at Jesus' life. Sure, he went off alone to pray, but the majority of his ministry was spent with people. He surrounded himself with a community of disciples. He interacted with and ministered to people all the time. And wasn't his life the holiest of lives?

God does not want you to be alone. Loneliness is not God's intention for you. In fact, the greatest miracles of healing seem to happen when people help one another.

A woman in our parish lost her husband unexpectedly. He went in for a simple heart procedure and did not survive. She was left suddenly and terribly alone. She came to my office one week after the funeral in a state of shock. Her family had dispersed, her friends were not constantly by her side, and she was afraid. She did not know how to continue to live, or if she even wanted to live.

The only remedy that I have ever found for grief is community. I listened to her pain and encouraged her to come to a grief support group that we offer at the church. Something powerful happens when the grieving share their pain with one another. Sharing eases loneliness, and though it doesn't remove despair, it helps people learn to live again.

I think that God often gives us to each other. God knows that some of the best, most loving ministry is done from one person to another. Christ acts most powerfully in and through us. He gives us each other to ease the pain. His compassion is expressed in community. If you are in pain, if you are grieving, don't let yourself be alone too much. Let others care for you. Surround yourself with people who care, who understand, who listen. Jesus would want you to do that.

Find Your Own Personal Way to Say, "The kingdom of God is near!"

Jesus came to Galilee, proclaiming the good news of God, and saying, "The time is fulfilled, and the kingdom of God is near!"

MARK 1:14–15

I am afraid these days. I watch the news and see a wedding party in Baghdad blown up during the taking of photos, and I get scared. When I get scared, I stick to routine. I harden my schedule with appointments and to-do lists so that I feel in control. I wake up in the morning, look at my schedule, and think that I know what will happen to me that day. The truth is that I have no idea what will happen when I step out my front door, but I ignore the truth and cling to my schedule.

Consistency is good for human beings. It makes us comfortable. When raising a child, all the books tell you to set up a routine and stick with it. Naps at a certain time, stories and prayers before bed; whatever it is, make it consistent, and your child will be comforted. Routine alleviates anxiety. It gives us the impression that we are in control of our lives.

The truth is, we should be afraid, because we are not in control and we have no idea what might happen to us today. Like the bride and groom in that Iraqi wedding party, we might die just when the photographer says "Cheese!" The road of discipleship is unpredictable. There can be no scheduling, no plans. You cannot expect to encounter God at a certain time, in a certain way. The road to discipleship belongs to God, and God alone has the map.

Jesus sent out seventy people ahead of him to the towns where he was expected to go. He did not prepare them. He did not give them schedules, itineraries, books to read, or speeches to deliver. He told them that they could not bring money. Can you imagine going on a trip without money? The first thing I do on my way to the airport is check to see if I have my wallet. Everything can be purchased, but you definitely don't want to leave home without money.

Yet, Jesus told them not to pack—no extra clothes, nothing. They were to be completely dependent on their hosts for their survival. And they had only one phrase that they were to repeat to everyone they encountered: *The kingdom of God is near!* For most of my adult life, I have been trying to figure out what Jesus meant by these words, and all I can come up with is this: *God is close.* It is an extraordinarily simple message. It is a message which can be translated many different ways. There are many ways of telling people that God is with them.

No matter how people responded, whether they welcomed the disciples or rejected them, the messengers were to say the same thing: *The kingdom of God is near!* I guess they were to tell this to everyone because no matter what you do, God is still around. There is nothing that we humans can do to get God to stop being present with us. Invited or not, God is here.

In his book, *A Long Way Gone*, Ishmael Beah tells the true story of his life as a child soldier in Sierra Leone. He tells of the near starvation that forced him to join the army, of the way he was taught to kill using a machine gun at the age of twelve, of his horror as he watched women and children shot to death, their bodies mangled, their blood seeping into the ground. After three or four years, Ishmael was taken to Freetown, where he was put in a rehabilitation hospital. There was a young woman nurse there who listened to him. He suffered from migraines and nightmares. He would lash out at the smallest provocation and become violent or sullen. All the while, she listened, responding to him over and over again with, "It's not your fault." *It's not your fault.* This was her way of telling him that God is near, that everything is okay, that the kingdom of God is at hand. This was her translation of the very same message.

At first, her words infuriated him. Then, they began to sink in, and he began to tell her more and more about the horrors he had seen and the horrors he had performed. She would say it again, "It's not your fault." Ishmael had to leave that place without ever telling her how much she meant to him, how much he loved her. Later, he would wonder how she did it. How could she listen to stories of horror with such patience? How could she stand it?

Jesus told his disciples that he would be coming after them. They were not responsible for the final outcome. They were to give the message and minister as best they could, but the rest would be God's doing. Only Jesus could clean up the mess. Perhaps this young woman knew her role. Perhaps that was what gave her the strength to listen and to tell war-ravaged children that the kingdom of God is near.

Forgive and Free Yourself

"Forgive us our sins,
as we forgive those who sin against us."

cf. LUKE 11:4

In the Lord's Prayer, Jesus directly links the forgiveness we have for others with the forgiveness God has for us. If we are to be saved, if we are to come to God and live eternally after death, we must learn to forgive in this life. There is no discipleship, no following of Jesus without forgiveness. It is a key ingredient in the Christian life.

The word Jesus used when he spoke of forgiveness means much more than we realize. Our English language sometimes fools us into thinking that forgiveness means condoning. It does not. Forgiveness does not mean *letting* something happen, pretending it *didn't* happen, or saying that something is okay when it is not. Forgiveness is not about allowing criminals to go unpunished or injustice to go untouched. Forgiveness is not about the wrongdoer; it is about the victim. Forgiveness means *to let go* or, perhaps more poignantly, *to set free*.

When the brokenness of our world surrounds us, we tend to cling. We cling to our belongings, we cling to money, and we cling to relationships—especially the broken ones. Think of when someone has unjustly wronged you. Does it bother you? Does the offense creep under your skin and begin to obsess you? Do you find yourself going over and over that relationship, the wrongs that were done, the lack of remorse, the hurt feelings? This kind of obsession can *consume* you. It will consume you if you don't learn how to set yourself free.

When I was in high school, I carried the groceries up the stairs for an elderly Jewish woman. She seemed grouchy all the time. After the last bag had been lifted onto her tiny kitchen counter, she would inevitably offer me a cookie and something to drink, and she would talk. She always talked about the same thing: her rotten sons.

This woman had two "boys" who did not call her. She refused to call them because they were "rotten," though she never specified how she came to this decisive opinion. She thought of them constantly, and as she moved closer to death, she clung to her disappointment and anger. Every day, every hour that proceeded without a phone call drove her deeper into misery. She was entirely wrapped up in her obsession with them.

Months later, she became ill with cancer. She was moved to an inpatient Hospice unit. I suggested that she call her boys. She refused. So my dad and I called them for her, and I will never forget the scene of their reunion. Her boys weren't boys at all. They were in their sixties. But you would have thought they were five years old, judging by the way they crept into that room, all sheepish and reticent.

"You ROTTEN, ROTTEN BOYS!" she yelled, "I've missed you SO MUCH!" And she burst into tears. They said how sorry they were, that they thought she was mad at them. "I was!" she said, "But you should have called me anyway."

There was a kind of light that seemed to burst into the room at that point, a dawning of understanding, a relaxation, a relief. It was visible forgiveness. I could see it on their faces. There were hugs, tears, and smiles. I was only in high school, but I have never forgotten the way things changed in that room. She died the next day. I think that all she needed to do was to let go.

If You've Run Away from God, Run Back

"Or what woman having ten silver coins, if she loses one of them, does not light a lamp, sweep the house, and search carefully until she finds it? When she has found it, she calls together her friends and neighbors, saying, 'Rejoice with me, for I have found the coin that I had lost.' Just so, I tell you, there is joy in the presence of the angels of God over one sinner who repents."

LUKE 15:8–10

The disciples all ran away when Jesus was threatened. It is only after they returned that they were able to become the people Jesus truly wanted them to be. They only became the Church when they returned and saw the resurrection and forgiveness of Christ.

Running away is an inevitable part of discipleship. There will come a time in each of our lives when things will get too hard and we will want to bolt. I have seen people run from God for many reasons. Sometimes they wander away, like my little two-year-old Max, who wandered off on the football field one day, causing my husband and me quite a scare. Sometimes people run because they feel that they have failed God. I see people quit committees or leave church, and often their decisions are based more on feelings of shame and guilt than on conflicts of interest or a sense of disappointment with others. Sometimes we run away because we are mad at God. When tragedy hits, and we don't understand what has happened, we flee.

When her son died, Kathy decided she wanted to die. Die or disappear—that's what she said. "I just want to drive and never return." Her pain was so great that she just wanted to end it all. And on top of her pain was the even stronger feeling of the injustice of it all. Her son had been disabled. He had been kind and pure of heart. How dare God end his life?

Kathy ran and ran, but God kept searching for her despite her fast flight. She gave up her job as a doctor and moved to the Mediterranean. One day, on the beach, God found her anyway. The sun was rising, and she was overcome with a peace she had never tasted before. It washed over her as the waves were washing over the shore. Then she knew that her son was well.

It is hard to imagine that God searches for us. After all the ways that we fail, after all the mistakes that we make, how could God possibly want us? But Jesus is very clear on this fact: God never stops looking for us. Like a woman searching for her lost coin, we are precious to God, and God will not stop until we are found.

I was rereading the creation story a few days ago when I realized something. In the Garden of Eden, when we ate of the fruit of the Tree of the Knowledge of Good and Evil, God did not expel us immediately. The first thing God did was to search for us. "Where are you?" God asked when we hid ourselves from shame. "Where are you?" and only then, "What have you done?" Since we had to leave the Garden of Eden as a consequence of our new knowledge, God clothed us. And don't you realize that the entire story of Scripture, ever since we left Eden, has been the story of God trying to find us again?

There is nothing we can do to make God stop loving us. Nothing. God will search for us to the end of time. So, like Jesus' disciples, even though we have abandoned him, if we let ourselves be found again, the Church begins.

Say the Important Stuff Before You Die

"Peace I leave with you; my peace I give to you. I do not give to you as the world gives. Do not let your hearts be troubled, and do not let them be afraid."

JOHN 14:27

Jesus was clear in his communication with his loved ones as he neared his death. At the end, he was still giving instructions and caring for others. If you were told that you had only hours to live, what would you do? How would you spend your time? Who would you want to see? Whatever you decide will shed enormous light on your true priorities, for you would want to do what was most important at such a vital time. Jesus chose to have a meal. He fed his disciples and joined them at the table.

At Barnes and Noble, the largest book section is the cookbooks. Isn't that strange? The cookbooks. There is something about food and humanity. Food is so vastly important to us.

Perhaps we will never be able to unpack the meaning behind the Last Supper. Why, with only hours of freedom left, did Jesus choose to eat with his friends? Why did he break bread and give it to them, telling them that it was his body? Such a strange, cannibalistic reference was totally foreign to the disciples. Why did he want them to eat his body and drink his blood?

Throughout his ministry, Jesus tried over and over again to explain God's love to us. He pounded us with parables about the kingdom of God, the forgiveness of God, and the grace of God. But we could not get it, even with repetition. Even through the simplest of metaphors, we could not get it. So instead, Jesus fed us.

I believe that the story of the Garden of Eden points to a deep truth about who we are as humans. We fell from God's grace through an act of consumption. We took the one fruit that was not freely given and, in doing so, became estranged from God, naked and alone. If Jesus could not explain salvation, he could at least give us the antidote to our disease. In the same way that a fish cannot identify the water in which it swims, we could not rationally comprehend our own sinfulness, but we could be fed. We could swallow the antidote, and God could bridge the gap of salvation for us.

An older woman in our parish was dying. Her daughter called, and I drove so fast to the house that a cop stopped me to give me a speeding ticket. When he found out that this woman, whom he happened to know, was dying, he drove me to her house. When I arrived, she was smiling. Thin as a rail, she was no longer eating or drinking. "She won't eat!" her daughter cried. "She won't let me feed her!" The daughter was panicky, but the woman was just doing what came naturally.

Her body was shutting down. She was preparing to die. Force-feeding her at this point would have only caused her pain. She needed to refrain from eating. But her inability to eat alarmed her daughter more than anything else.

At a primal level, food is life. When we don't eat, we die. Jesus wanted us to live, to live longer and deeper than we can comprehend. He wanted us to join him in eternity. What better way to show us than to feed us, to give us life through food? In feeding us, Jesus was reassuring us that he wanted us to live. This was, quite literally, the food of eternal life.

Don't Run Away from the Dying; Run to Them

After these things, Joseph of Arimathea, who was a disciple of Jesus, though a secret one because of his fear of the Jews, asked Pilate to let him take away the body of Jesus. Pilate gave him permission; so he came and removed his body.

JOHN 19:38

When I was a child, we would pass by a graveyard on the way to summer camp. When passing the graves, I had been told to hold my breath. It was bad luck to breathe when passing graves. You had to hide your breath inside you. I never asked why. All I remember is the gray stones whizzing by while my lungs ached.

Most people run from pain, conflict, and death. We just find it too hard to face these things head on, so we sidle along in life, flinching at the words "he died" or "she has cancer." We flinch because it is bad news and because it scares us.

A woman whose son died in a car crash was amazed by how many people didn't ask her about him at all. They would come up to her at cocktail parties and comment on her dress, the weather, her other children perhaps, but never about her son. She had so many friends before the accident. After her son died, everyone was nice to her; they showered her with gifts and cards, but gradually she found that they drifted away. One day, over lunch, she dared to ask a friend why she never asked about her son's accident. "Oh, I didn't want to remind you of it!" she said, as if the mother could think of anything else.

When it comes to matters of dying, we avoid them like crazy. One man who is on hospice care does not even want a funeral. "I don't want people thinking about my death! I want them to think of me alive!" he said. When his wife tries to talk about his death, he refuses to listen. "I will not discuss it," he says.

We speak of *passing away* instead of dying. Funeral homes use fake grass to hide the dirt of the grave. In my tradition, I am to place dirt on the coffin during the burial service while I say, "Earth to earth, ashes to ashes, dust to dust." Funeral directors often give me fake sand instead of dirt. I have to request real dirt! One man even asked, "Where do I get some for you?" "It's all around us!" I said.

Often at funerals, the family will leave before the casket is lowered into the ground. It is too hard to see the fake grass pulled back and the true darkness of the hole in the ground. It is too devastating. They find it intolerable. Not everyone walks away, but most do. Everyone leaves, and these manual laborers appear out of nowhere. After pulling the fake grass off like plastic rugs, they use ropes or belts to lower the coffin into the ground. It is an awkward thing to do, but I try to stay, to see it all.

When Jesus died on the cross, his body would have been left to hang there to be eaten by the buzzards. Crosses were like the worst kind of billboard. Just outside the city walls, men hung naked, their flesh slowly torn apart by buzzards, a horrible reminder of what happened when you disobeyed Roman law. Like the bodies of the two other criminals, Jesus' body would have been left on the cross to rot, but someone courageous came to retrieve it.

Joseph of Arimathea was a man of wealth. He was organized enough to have made a tomb for himself, complete with a huge rock to roll in front to contain the stench of decay. Joseph also had courage. Instead of running away from Jesus' death, he went to retrieve the body. The Romans did not have to give it to him. They could have refused; they could have turned on him. By requesting Jesus' body, Joseph was exposing himself as a member of a dangerous messianic movement. He could have avoided the whole thing. He could have mourned Jesus in private as most of the disciples did, but he chose to face the Romans, request the body of Jesus, and take it down from the cross. Joseph faced the horror of a decaying body. He loved Jesus that much.

Reflection Questions for Chapter 7

1. Are you afraid to talk about dying?
   Can you begin to talk about it with the people you love?

2. What is your way of saying that the kingdom of God is near, your way of saying that God is around?

3. When have you run away from God?
   How did you come back?

CHAPTER 8

Prepare for Eternal Life

Easter Week

.

Love

When the sabbath was over, Mary Magdalene, and Mary the mother of James, and Salome bought spices, so that they might go and anoint Jesus.

MARK 16:1

We can learn a great deal from the women who approached the tomb after Jesus' death. They came early on Easter morning. They were not allowed to come on the Sabbath, but as soon as it was daylight, they came. They brought spices with them to anoint Jesus' body.

Think of what they were facing. Most likely, there would be a large stone in front of the grave. How did they plan on moving it? Would they be strong enough? If they succeeded, there would most likely be a terrible stench. And darkness. They would have to walk into a dark cave, looking for a dead body. They were prepared to see the body of their teacher, bloodied and stiff. All this they faced because they loved him.

Even in his resurrection, Jesus was teaching us. It is not a coincidence that the ones who were willing to face the darkness were the first to see the light. The Resurrected Jesus first came to those who were willing to face death itself. There is only one way to end pain, and that is to face it and move through it. These women were willing to suffer to see the truth. And the truth was far greater than they could have ever imagined.

I have always found it to be of vital importance that Jesus only appeared in resurrected form to those who loved him. He appeared to the disciples, to the women, to those who longed to see him. What if no one had loved Jesus? If no one had loved him, we might have missed his resurrection entirely. If no one had loved him, we might not have the message of eternal life, the greatest miracle of all time. The miracle of salvation is entirely dependent on love.

Jesus' resurrection is what changed everything. Even with all the miracles that he performed, if Jesus had not risen from the dead, no one would have known of him. He would have faded into oblivion along with hundreds of other itinerant preachers. His love of God, his parables, and his teachings would have been lost in the morass of time.

It was only after the resurrection that people began to go back and reflect upon Jesus' life. The first Christian writings were not the Gospels, but the letters of Paul, telling people of Jesus' marvelous resurrection and what it meant for all who believed. It was not until the disciples were dying that people began to see the need to write down accounts of Jesus' life. If he was the Son of God, then how did he spend his time? What did he do for us? How did he live? We only became fascinated with his life after he rose from the dead. So all would have been lost to us if no one had loved him. It all hinged on love. Doesn't it always?

There is no way to find God but by loving. We cannot understand God, nor can we behave rightly. But we can love. It is our heart that saves us.

Touch Peace

"Peace be with you."

JOHN 20:19

When the resurrected Christ appeared in the Upper Room, he repeated himself. He said, "Peace be with you;" not once, not twice, but three times. Why not just say "Hi" or "Here I am" or "I am with you"? Why did he choose to say, *Peace be with you?* Was there some significance to these words?

It makes me wonder what things looked like for Jesus after the resurrection. He had died and risen again. He had traveled to God and then returned to us, fully conscious of this journey. He saw everything from the perspective of heaven, and still, the first thing he says to the gathered disciples is, *Peace be with you.* His wish for us is that we find peace.

From God's perspective, we must look very troubled. Ever since the fall of humankind from God's grace, we have been trying to do things our way, a decision that has resulted in great suffering. There is no adequate translation for the Hebrew word, *shalom.* Most of us imagine peace to be merely the absence of conflict. But I believe it is so much more than that.

Peace is the state in which God exists in absolute harmony with the universe. Peace cannot be described, rather it must be experienced.

A woman I worked with years ago suffered from terrible clinical depression. No amount of therapy or medication seemed to help. She found herself so lost that she couldn't get out of bed for months. She would hide under her covers in bed and cry, trying to will herself out of existence.

Once, in the middle of the night, she was curled up under her covers weeping uncontrollably when something happened. She did not see anything or hear anything, but a feeling of incredible peace washed over her. She had no idea where it came from. It came as an inexpressibly beautiful and comforting gift. The peace that was given to her changed her whole life. She was able to get out of bed. She was able to function. She continued to have struggles, but, whenever she felt lost, she would meditate and return to the peacefulness that had been given to her. For the rest of her life, the feeling never dissipated or disappeared. It remained potent and present to her. Just a drop of God's peace lasted a lifetime.

At the end of our Sunday services, I say this ancient blessing:

> *May the Peace of God, which passes all understanding,*
> *keep your hearts and minds in the knowledge and*
> *love of God and of his Son, Jesus Christ.*

That is what he came back to give us, *peace.*

Just Witness the Glory

When Judas had gone out, Jesus said, "Now the Son of Man has been glorified, and God has been glorified in him. If God has been glorified in him, God will also glorify him in himself and will glorify him at once. Little children, I am with you only a little longer. You will look for me; and as I said to the Jews so now I say to you, 'Where I am going, you cannot come.' I give you a new commandment, that you love one another. Just as I have loved you, you also should love one another. By this everyone will know that you are my disciples, if you have love for one another."

JOHN 13:31-35

A tornado hit a small town west of us. The front page of this morning's paper showed a panoramic view; there was nothing left. The trees looked like sticks. The houses were simply demolished. I can only imagine what it must have been like to have lived through such an ordeal, to have heard the sirens and taken cover and afterwards discover that your home is gone. One elderly woman said that her entire life was blown away. She had nothing left.

This morning I had to usher an entire congregation downstairs to the basement. Sirens went off all over town. After the sirens ceased, we came upstairs and worshiped, but I had a reliable lawyer sit in the office just off the sanctuary listening to the radio. At any moment, he might have given me a signal, and I would have ushered 150 people downstairs again. The elderly had a hard time with the stairs, but the storm passed us by.

Why does Greensburg get demolished, and Wichita just get rain? These kind of catastrophes bring up the big questions: Why does God do this to us? Does God allow bad things to happen? Why? Does God even care? It seems there is no adequate answer to what I now call the *why*-question. I get asked it all the time. All my adult life I have struggled to find an answer that satisfies, but I find none. I simply cannot understand.

Jesus never once commanded us to understand God. I believe that he knew that comprehension of the divine was impossible for human beings. Instead, he keeps repeating the word, *glory*. In the Gospel of John, he uses this word over and over again. The Father will glorify the Son, the Son will glorify the Father, and *we* are supposed to glorify God.

In the ancient Greek of the New Testament, the word *glory* literally means *brightness*. It is as though God possesses a quality of brightness so magnificent that we cannot look at it directly. Glory suggests the brilliance of the sun, which would easily blind us. We cannot get our minds around God, but we can witness to God's magnificence, God's brightness.

A few weeks ago, I saw an incredible rainbow. After I pulled into the parking lot of the church, I stepped out of my car, and there it was. It was the most magnificent rainbow I have ever seen. It arched from one end of the sky to the other. It was so beautiful, so bright, that I couldn't just stand there. I ran inside and interrupted a grief support group. Someone was crying, but I told them to run outside. They did, and they couldn't believe its beauty. Then I rounded up another class to witness the glory. I then ran into the kitchen and found a woman cleaning. When she and I arrived outside, the rainbow had gone. She looked at me like I had lost my mind.

All that Jesus asks of us is to witness God's glory. We may never understand it in this lifetime, but we can still witness the brightness of glory. Jesus says that he will be glorified in the cross. That means that we can glorify God in pain. We glorify God when we love despite hardship and despair—a strange concept, but I see it carried out every day. Perhaps that is the greatest kind of glory, when we can point out the brightness of God even in the midst of our own pain.

My friend who is a deacon has a malignant brain tumor. His portacath protrudes out of his head. He wonders why this has happened to him at a time in his life when he feels called to do so much ministry, but he has chosen to glorify God in his last few days rather than dwell on his misfortune. Last weekend, I helped him baptize his grandson. His thin frame could hardly lift the boy, but he managed it. It was a sight even more beautiful than the rainbow.

Maybe Jesus was trying to show us that the purpose of this life is not to understand, but merely to glorify God. To glorify God in the beauty and in the sadness, in the light and in the dark, to glorify God even in the cross itself.

Laugh

Jesus said to them, "Children, you have no fish, have you?"

JOHN 21:5

When Jesus appears after his crucifixion, he plays a game. The disciples have returned home to the Sea of Galilee because they don't know what else to do. What do you do when you followed a teacher across the country, devoted your life to him, and now he is gone? How do you feel when your master is brutally, suddenly, and unexpectedly killed? Out of your despair and depression, you probably cling to the only things you have left: home and routine.

I can just picture the disciples sitting together in silence absorbed in their thoughts when Peter blurts out, "I'm going fishing." After all, that's what he used to do for a living. What else was there to do? The other disciples decide to go with him. They fish all night (fishermen still fish at night on the Sea of Galilee because that is when the fish rise), but they catch nothing, not a single bite. It must have been a dull night.

As the sun begins to rise, dancing and playing its rays over the twinkling water, Jesus appears on the shore. He calls out,

"Cast the net to the right side of the boat" (John 21:6). This is *exactly* how he called some of his disciples three years ago. I bet he had a huge smile on his face as he wondered how long it was going to take them to figure out it was him. When the net is overflowing with fish, the beloved disciple recognizes him. "It is the Lord!" (21:7). Then Peter, bless his soul, throws on his clothes (it was disrespectful to appear naked before a teacher) and leaps into the water.

I can just see Jesus laughing as Peter, soaking from head to toe, appears on the shore. And then Jesus feeds them. He's always feeding them! But this time, it's not the last meal of the day; it's the first meal. It's breakfast, the meal of hope.

I believe that Jesus laughed. I believe that he experienced joy and that his laughter was perhaps more important than his words. Not only was he physically alive, he was mentally well. He was not depressed, mourning, victimized, or traumatized. He was laughing. . . . He was laughing.

Wake Up Now

Then their eyes were opened, and they recognized him.

LUKE 24:31a

Cleopas and another disciple had to *get out of Dodge*. They had too much to process after Jesus' death: their failure to stand with him, their disappointment with how it all ended, and the crazy rumors that he had reappeared. They needed to get out of town to walk and talk. Sometimes I need to do that, too. When something bad happens to me, when I need to think or talk with my husband, I get into my car and drive. Some of our best conversations have been in the car, looking at the road and talking about whatever comes to mind.

These two disciples were having one of these therapeutic conversations when a stranger came up and asked them what they were talking about. "Where have you been?" they say. Everybody had heard about the crucifixion. Didn't this guy read the papers? How ignorant could you be? So they poured out the story. They told him about how much they loved Jesus, how they had hoped he was the Messiah, and how he died.

"You are fools," the man said. "Don't you read the Bible?" He then proceeded to interpret the Scriptures for them in a way that they had never thought of before. He told them about Isaiah who, seven hundred years ago, told of how God would give a Son to the world who was destined to suffer; he told them about Ezekiel, who spoke of a shepherd who would lead his flock; and about Daniel, who had nighttime visions of a man who would come in glory and whose kingdom would not pass away. As the man spoke, they began to realize that the Scriptures had told of a different kind of Messiah than they had imagined, a Messiah whom Jesus did indeed represent.

When the disciples reached their destination, Emmaus, they didn't want the conversation to end. They invited the man inside. It is customary for the guest to break the bread, so the stranger did, saying the *berakah*, the blessing over the bread:

> *Blessed are you, Lord God of the Universe,*
> *for you bring forth bread from the earth.*

The disciples woke up, and they suddenly recognized that this stranger was Jesus. And just as suddenly, he was gone.

Why did they not know him when he was explaining the Scriptures to them? What planet were they on? How could they have walked and talked with him and not have known? It was only when he broke the bread that they could let go of their processing and planning and become fully present.

If you want to find the living Christ, you cannot find him in the past, and you will not be able to see him in the future.

The only place to find him is *now*, in this very moment. You can only find him now. The key, then, to loving God is to learn to live in the present, to be fully awake. People have been trying to do this for thousands of years, in all of the major world religions—to be fully awake *now* and, in that way, to find God.

If you want to be well, you must first live in the here and now. In this very moment, not dwelling on past mistakes and not absorbed with your plans for the future. You must see Christ in this very moment. This is the only place that you can find Him.

Playing Before God

> *Jesus sat down, called the twelve, and said to them, "Whoever*
> *wants to be first must be last of all and servant of all." Then he*
> *took a little child and put it among them; and taking it in his*
> *arms, he said to them, "Whoever welcomes one such child in my*
> *name welcomes me, and whoever welcomes me welcomes not me*
> *but the one who sent me."*

MARK 9:35–37

My son Max, who is four, is playing soccer with his buddies
this season, and I am blessed to be the coach of their preschool soccer team. Soccer with preschoolers is like a comedy
of errors. One kid does not want to step on any ants (because
that would be killing), so he tiptoes across the field. One girl
likes to do ballet on the field during the game. My friend's son
will run up and down the field screaming, "It's my turn! It's
my turn!," but he never gets the ball. Another boy decides to
pick a flower in the middle of the game or score a goal in his
own goal and watch all the grown ups yell and get red in the
face as they try to get him to turn around. One kid loves to
score, so whenever he gets the ball he just drives it right down

the field and into the goal. BOOM! He did this six times in a row in the last game, and a little boy on the other team burst into tears and ran off the field!

And here I am, the coach, trying to convince them to score as many goals as possible. "Score!" I yell; "Run!" I scream. Trying to get them to run in the right direction is like herding cats. Sometimes, though, I will stop yelling and just laugh. A thought will come across my mind. *Why am I telling them to score? Is it so important to win the game, to get the most points? What if the little ballerina has it right?*

Jesus tells us that, when it comes to God, we've got it all backwards. We think that the point of life is to score the most goals, to be successful and to gain respect. But that is not the point of life at all. We can never earn our way to heaven. No, God wants us to play, to love, to stop and smell the flowers.

If we want to grow closer to God, we must rewind back to preschool and remember how to play. We must go back to the days when there were no cliques and no judgments, when kids hugged each other and got really excited about a little spider that found its way onto the windowsill. We must open our eyes to the bubbles that float in the sky when you blow on a stick dipped in soap. We must see the colors of a radiant sunset.

Each Sunday, we ask a small child to bring a basket up to our altar in church. The children fill this basket with what they call their *thanksgivings*. These can be coins—some of them tithe their allowance—or it might be a leaf they found, or a picture they made. When they carry up their gifts, I find it so beautiful. The little child reaching up to the towering altar handing the small things that he has made or collected is an icon for me. When it comes to God, none of us can earn our way. We are all children, standing before the majesty of our Maker, lifting up our hands with our tiny gifts. Don't forget that you are a child of God. To find God, you must learn to play, to stand in awe and give thanks.

A Parting Gift

> *"If you love me, you will keep my commandments. And I will ask the Father, and he will give you another Advocate, to be with you forever. This is the Spirit of truth. . . ."*

> JOHN 14:15–17a

People ask me *why*-questions all the time.

> *Why did God let my son die?*
> *Why do I have cancer?*
> *Why does God allow the world to be such a mess?*
> *Why doesn't God come and solve some of our problems?*
> *Why can't I understand?*

I sit there in my office like a bump on a log. I listen. And I cannot give these people the answers they deserve. I wonder if God wants them to understand or if it's just not possible. God is more real to me than the chair in which I sit, but I cannot explain why God does anything. I simply do not understand. And I can't help but wonder, is it possible for any of us to understand?

Jesus once told us that he wanted to explain everything. He wanted to let us in on it all, but he couldn't because we could not tolerate the entirety of God's presence. We could not bear to witness too much of God. It was simply too much for us—too bright, too brilliant, too good, too much. God does not answer all of our questions; that is true. But it is not because God withholds from us. Our questions are left unanswered because we are unable to tolerate the answers.

Moses could not look at God because God was too bright. He had to look at the backside of God or, more specifically, at where God just was. Even the most devout person cannot tolerate that much of God. It is simply too much: too much holiness, too much goodness, too much truth. It is like looking directly at the sun.

I believe that the Holy Spirit is a way to titrate God's presence. It is God's attempt to give us glimpses slowly and only when we are ready. The Holy Spirit is a gift, a gift of infinite patience and understanding. All will be revealed to us, but only when we are ready.

When I was a little girl, my parents went through a rough patch in their marriage. They fought loudly and often, breaking dishes and hollering. I remember their fights. One day, at nursery school, I decided to hide in my cubby. I remember what it felt like. I had just put my jacket and my lunch box inside the cubby. I looked inside. It looked so quiet, so safe in there. I hid inside, thinking that maybe the world could go on without me. I liked it in there. It felt safe. I could hear myself breathe. The fighting couldn't fit in there; just me, and the quiet, and the cramped smell of my lunch box. My nursery school teacher couldn't get me to come out that day. Evidently, she called my parents. She recommended that I see a child psychologist. My parents diligently obeyed. The psychologist's name was Dr. Wolfe. I remember that there was a large banister going up to Dr. Wolfe's room. She was a gentle, older woman with dark hair. I remember that she played with me and listened to me. We drew pictures. She smiled. When I was done with my sessions, she gave me a cupcake. I still remember the cupcake.

Dr. Wolfe did not describe the nature of anxiety to my four-year-old self. She did not explain to me about the fear of abandonment. She just played, and she listened. She followed my lead, letting me play games. If I wanted to be the princess, I got to be the princess, and she dutifully played the monster bad-guy. We drew pictures. All the time, while we were playing, she was gently asking me questions, nudging me into new ways of thinking. She was my friend. She met me where I was, in my four-year-old world of fear, and she showed me the way out of the cubby hole, into something bigger.

The Holy Spirit is a lot like Dr. Wolfe. I believe that the Spirit listens to us a great deal. The Spirit meets us where we are, and then gently nudges us in the right direction. The Spirit is always inviting us to play, but we are often so busy and self-consumed that we do not respond. And so the Spirit waits until we can listen a little better. The Spirit nudges and listens, waits and plays.

I do not believe that God is in a hurry. But I do believe that God wants us to know everything, and that God waits patiently for us to become ready to receive the truth. We begin the journey by admitting what we do not know. We begin by realizing that we are small children in the eyes of God, trapped in boxes of routine and self-definition, pattern and neurosis. We begin by admitting that we do not understand much at all.

Wouldn't it be wonderful if the religious leaders of the world could begin to discuss what we *don't* know as opposed to fighting over what we *do* know? Could we have more peace if we admitted that we all are like lost children before the magnificence of God? If you do not understand much, that is a good place to begin. It is your own limitations that prevent you from understanding God, not God's refusal to communicate. There is nothing that God wants more than to communicate with you.

Reflection Questions for Chapter 8

1. What do you love most about your life?
   Who do you love? How can you increase that love?

2. How can you wake up and see the glory each day?
   What would be some steps that you could take to
   get more aware of God's presence in your life?

Conclusion

Years ago, I traveled to Israel with my husband. We spent a month traveling throughout the regions of the Galilee, Jerusalem, and even the Sinai desert. On the day before we were to leave, we watched the sun set on the Sea of Galilee. I walked amidst the rushes by the shore. The wind was blowing, and the light from the setting sun danced on the water. I almost thought I could see Jesus. Wasn't he right around the corner? If only I concentrated hard enough, maybe Jesus would appear by the shore to me as he did to Peter, laughing at my shock and surprise.

I didn't see Jesus that day, though I believe that he was there. But I realized then and there that I would spend my life trying to see Him. This book is just one more attempt to find him and, in finding him, to discover that he has taught me how to be well—mentally, spiritually, and psychologically well. This is a devotional book. I hope that, in reading it, you have found yourself wanting to see Jesus, too.

Additional Praise

"Kate Moorehead's insights into sin offer a refreshing mirror in which we can see ourselves, not in some punishing, medieval fashion—but as precious children of Christ's redemption. She looks deeply into the reality of sin, faces it squarely and produces fresh insights that are both positive and life changing for those whose lens for seeing God is Jesus Christ."

The Rev. Dr. Mark S. Anschutz
Parish Consultant, Clergy Coach, Preacher and Teacher